OFFICE SYSTEMS:
Planning, Procurement and Implementation

ELLIS HORWOOD SERIES IN COMPUTERS AND THEIR APPLICATIONS

Series Editor: Brian Meek, Director of the Computer Unit, Queen Elizabeth College, University of London

Atherton, R.	**Structured Programming with COMAL**
Berry, R. E.	**Programming Language Translation**
Brailsford, D. F. and Walker, A. N.	**Introductory ALGOL 68 Programming**
Bull, G. M.	**The Dartmouth Time Sharing System**
Burns, A.	**New Information Technology**
Burns, A.	**The Microchip: Appropriate or Inappropriate Technology**
Cope, T.	**Computing using BASIC: An Interactive Approach**
Dahlstrand, I.	**Software Portability and Standards**
Davie, F. J. T. and Morrison, R.	**Recursive Descent Compiling**
Deasington, R. J.	**A Practical Guide to Computer Communications and Networking Second Edition**
Deasington, R. J.	**X.25 Explained**
Ennals, R.	**Logic Programmers and Logic Programming**
Fossum, E.	**Computerization of Working Life**
Gray, P. M. D.	**Logic, Algebra and Databases**
Harland, D. M.	**Polymorphic Programming Languages**
Hill, I. D. and Meek, B. L.	**Programming Language Standardisation**
Hutchison, D.	**Fundamentals of Computer Logic**
McKenzie, J., Elton, L. and Lewis, R.	**Interactive Computer Graphics in Science Teaching**
Matthews, J.	**FORTH**
Meek, B. L., Fairthorne, S. and Moore, L.	**Using Computers, 2nd Edition**
Meek, B. L., Heath, P. and Rushby, N.	**Guide to Good Programming Practice, 2nd Edition**
Millington, D.	**Systems Analysis and Design for Computer Application**
Moore, L.	**Foundations of Programming with PASCAL**
Paterson, A.	**Word Processing and the Automated Office**
Pesaran, H. M. and Slater, L. J.	**Dynamic Regression: Theory and Algorithms**
Peter, R.	**Recursive Functions in Computer Theory**
Ramsden, E.	**Microcomputers in Education 2**
Sharp, J. A.	**Data Flow Computing**
Smith, I. C. H.	**Microcomputers in Education**
Spath, H.	**Cluster Analysis Algorithms**
Spath, H.	**Cluster Dissection and Analysis**
Stratford-Collins, M. J.	**ADA: A Programmer's Conversion Course**
Teskey, F. N.	**Principles of Text Processing**
Turner, S. J.	**An Introduction to Compiler Design**
Young, S. J.	**An Introduction to ADA, Second (Revised) Edition**
Young, S. J.	**Real Time Languages**

ELLIS HORWOOD BOOKS IN COMPUTING

Series Editor: A. J. Jones, Brunel University

Atherton, R.	**Structured Programming with BBC BASIC**
Barrett, T. P. and Colwill, S.	**Winning Games on the Commodore 64**
Barrett, T. P. and Jones, A. J.	**Winning Games on the VIC-20**
Christensen, B.	**Beginning COMAL**
Cole, D. G. J.	**Getting Started on the ORIC-1**
Cotton, K. et al.	**Information Technology and the New Generation**
Ennals, R.	**Beginning micro-PROLOG, 2nd Revised Edition**
Goodyear, P.	**Commodore 64 LOGO**
Goodyear, P.	**LOGO: A Guide to Learning through Programming**
Hepburn, P.	**Problem-Solving with micro-PROLOG**
Jones, A. J. and Carpenter, G.	**Mastering the Commodore 64**
Jones, A. J., Coley, E. A. and Cole, D. G. J.	**Mastering the VIC-20**
Matthews, T. and Smith, P.	**Winning Games on the ZX Spectrum**
Matthews, T. and Smith, P.	**Winning Strategy Games on the Commodore 64**
Moore, L.	**Mastering the ZX Spectrum**
Narayanan, A.	**Beginning LISP**
Simon and Matthews, J.	**Mastering the Electron**

OFFICE SYSTEMS:
Planning, Procurement and Implementation

ALAN PATERSON, M.A.
Consultancy Director and Senior Partner
Charles Saunders Partnership, Norwich and Swanley, England

ELLIS HORWOOD LIMITED
Publishers · Chichester
Halsted Press: a division of
JOHN WILEY & SONS
Chichester · New York · Ontario · Brisbane

First published in 1985 by

ELLIS HORWOOD LIMITED
Market Cross House, Cooper Street, Chichester, West Sussex, PO19 1EB, England

The publisher's colophon is reproduced from James Gillison's drawing of the ancient Market Cross, Chichester.

Distributors:

Australia, New Zealand, South-east Asia:
Jacaranda-Wiley Ltd., Jacaranda Press,
JOHN WILEY & SONS INC.,
G.P.O. Box 859, Brisbane, Queensland 40001, Australia

Canada:
JOHN WILEY & SONS CANADA LIMITED
22 Worcester Road, Rexdale, Ontario, Canada.

Europe, Africa:
JOHN WILEY & SONS LIMITED
Baffins Lane, Chichester, West Sussex, England.

North and South America and the rest of the world:
Halsted Press: a division of
JOHN WILEY & SONS
605 Third Avenue, New York, N.Y. 10016, U.S.A.

British Library Cataloguing in Publication Data
Paterson, Alan
Office Systems: Planning, Procurement and Implementation –
(Ellis Horwood series in computers and their applications)
1. Word processing
I. Title
652'.5 HF5548.115

ISBN 0-85312-743-3 (Ellis Horwood Limited)
ISBN 0-470-20147-9 (Halsted Press)

Typeset by Ellis Horwood Limited.
Printed in Great Britain by R.J. Acford, Chichester.

Contents

Introduction

Looking at information handling in the mid-1980s, it no longer makes business sense to think separately of words and numbers, pictures and speech. All of these are used to convey information between human beings, and technology is rapidly making it possible to integrate this flow of knowledge at the office desk. Distinctions in technical terminology are also becoming increasingly blurred, removing demarcation lines which perhaps should never have been drawn. Data, text, voice and image processing are increasingly treated as sub-sets of information processing.

In the same way 'Office technology', a short-life buzzword coined originally to mean mainly word processing and directly related sub-systems, has become conceptually more global, embracing all computer-supported work in offices. It may reasonably be argued that anything a manager wants to achieve in office information handling, whether as end user or implementer of systems for others, may now be achieved with computer support. Whether that support is the most cost-effective way of achieving corporate objectives, or if there may be better options than computerising a system which has demonstrated its inability to cope, is a matter for another discipline – Organization and Methods (O&M) – which seems sadly to have disappeared (or even declared itself redundant) in many recent waves of organizational cost-cutting.

Capture of information can now be achieved in a variety of ways, using:

- conventional keyboard and screen
- variant keyboards (pressure pad, light occlusion, Maltron, etc.)
- touch-sensitive screens
- vector-plotting pens, mice and joysticks
- optical character/mark recognition
- manuscript recognition
- image scanners
- voice recognition.

Processing is no longer a matter of deciding whether a mainframe or mini should be used, but simply where microchip power needs to be applied, and whether input needs to be treated serially or by arrayed processors working in parallel, for the sake of optimal speed.

Storage and retrieval of information can be achieved more easily and economically with new mass-storage devices, ranging from five million-character Winchester-technology hard disks now available with even home computers, up to the massive 30,000 million characters promised for the latest jukebox-type unit with 15 optical disks. The difficulty lies increasingly not so much with finding ways to store information at costs many times cheaper than on paper, but rather how to design new indexing systems to address the vast masses of knowledge in an orderly form and with reasonable response times.

Display technology is constantly improving, and some of the latest portable terminals use flat-screen liquid crystal displays able to handle anything the traditional cathode ray tube can, but using comparatively trivial amounts of energy and taking up no physical space other than the glass they are mounted on. New bit-mapping displays offer graphical resolution and character/image mixing of great flexibility.

A quite amazing range of office print devices is currently available, ranging from the £50 Sinclair printer, and a £100 Japanese pocket device offering four-colour graphics up to sophisticated laser printers capable of improving on typesetters, for around £12–15,000 (and descending). At the upper end of the range, many of the new devices will double (soon) as coded-character printers and Group IV compatible facsimile receivers, making it possible to handle another organization's input on the same printer used for output from the receiving organization's computer systems.

Telecommunications options open to management are now constrained virtually only by carrier tariffs and standards for intercommunication between unlike devices; even standards are improving, especially with Teletex and the emerging Graphics Kernel, specifying how basic graphics elements shall be encoded for transmission.

Technology is a major driving force in systems integration; this is seen at present most clearly with the hybrid coded-character/facsimile printers described above, where microchip, laser/LED and photocopier technology, allied to facsimile and photosetting techniques, come together. In the software field, development of concurrent run-time operating systems such as C/CP/M for personal computing open up vast new areas of potential for allowing a single work-station to perform many different types of task in the same real time.

Information Retrieval and Database Management techniques have continued to move closer to each other, and we may shortly be in sight of a highly relational, but free-text oriented retrieval system suitable for running on a large micro, as the electronic filing cabinet.

Significant recent improvements in device portability mean that working from home, aboard planes, trains or ships is now a very real possibility, always provided that carriers make commercially available technically proven technology to capture moving signals; the home telephone will do nicely for 'cottaging' – working from home. Personal computers will be on the market in 1985 which weigh less than three pounds, have 20 million characters of non-mechanical storage, full 80-character × 25-line LCD displays and a motherboard able to hold at least two powerful microprocessors. They will probably not cost more than about £1,500 complete with standard interfaces and built-in modems.

Will this mean the beginning of the end for the paper factory which we all take the word 'office' to imply: the place of work rather than its original meaning, the job worked at? Or will managers, professionals and secretaries still prefer to commute to the paper-works, or at least as far as a local-area sub-set of it?

For those charged with delivering the electronic office, the choice is bewildering. All systems tend to seem equally attractive when smoothly demonstrated; inadequate solutions are frequently bought because of the odd function or facility which superficially distinguishes the preferred choice from a host of well-qualified options. The only sure way to avoid the hidden dangers and deficiencies is to resort to the classic traditions of O&M, and study the functional requirement in depth.

Another danger is that of re-inventing the wheel, represented in the case of office technology by expensive outlay on design of a new sytem which could have been obtained for a fraction of the price, with limited customization. Nobody's application is as esoteric as they tend to think, and somebody is almost sure to have covered a good part of the ground already. If they *haven't*, any decision to invest in development should then take into account the possibility of vending part or all of the resulting systems design as a packaged product to non-competing organizations with similar needs.

Pursuing the state of the art for its own sake is a good way to miss out on opportunities offered by current levels of proven technology. Two things are worth bearing in mind when dealing with the hard front edge of new technology:

(1) you have to start somewhere; technology of which others already have beneficial experience can't be the worst place to start;
(2) pioneers have always been identifiable by the feathered shafts between their shoulder-blades.

Like 'pioneering', another dangerous term to watch for is 'user-friendly'. Very few systems are, and most suppliers mean by this term that the end user will get used to it sooner or later, with luck and considerable effort. Non-technical users, who constitute the vast majority of staff affected by office computerization, cannot be expected to love the machine and integrate with it like cyborgs. They need encouragement, sympathetic training and, above all, the ability to change the way a machine works for them, rather than vice versa.

Finally, what's in IT for the user of 1984 and beyond?

Office technology will certainly hold down basic costs of handling information, particularly in paper document production. But these typically are only the tip of the overhead iceberg; the real savings are to be made in regrettably less quantifiable areas of benefit. New methodologies are needed, tailored to meet the specific objectives of the user organization, looking not only at direct cost savings, but more particularly at improvements in information quality (speed, accuracy, completeness), direct effects on the ability to generate revenue by handling substantially more business activity, savings in management time and stress, and generally perceptible overall enhancement of working conditions.

This book seeks to describe what can be achieved cost-effectively within a reasonable timescale in the office of 1984–85, placing considerable emphasis on word processing as the starting-point for electronic information handling. It then goes on to outline the wider attractions of office automation, and sets out guidelines for planning strategically and justifying tactically the progressive computerization of all office information handling.

ACKNOWLEDGEMENTS

I would like to express my gratitude to John Wells, Administrateur-General of Logica SA, Belgium for his valuable contribution in checking and making material comments on the first draft version of my book.

I thank both Logica/VTS and Penta Systems UK for supplying photographs.

1

What is word processing?

In 20 years' currency, the phrase 'word processing' has meant many things, and continues to be susceptible of a wide variety of interpretations. Etymologically, it would appear to derive from the German 'Textverarbeitung', which should have arrived in English as 'text processing', another very broadly interpreted computer industry catch-word.

Perhaps significantly for the electronic office of the future, the German coiners of the phrase gave it a broad definition embracing all text handling activities in offices. Headed by typing, these included facsimile transmission, audio dictation, telex, filing, printing and micrographics;

While some will hold the English phrase 'text processing' should more correctly embrace all these activities, leaving 'word processing' to mean simply computer-supported typing, the other end of the definitional range can be very narrow indeed.

In F. N. Teskey's book on text processing (*Principles of Text Processing,* Ellis Horwood, 1982) for example, the phrase 'word processing' is used only once and is not in the index; the book concentrates primarily on storage and retrieval of information from computer-supported textual databases.

In *this* book, 'word processing' is taken to mean computerized text capture (i.e. mainly typing), with built-in logical provisions for conceptual expansion from the key WP activities to others in the integrated office of the future, in which the semantic value of the phrase will have been reflated to mean what its German inventors had in mind.

1.1 DEFINITION OF THE WP SYSTEM

Strictly speaking, even a quill pen might be defined as a word processor, being the instrument by which an individual's thought can be processed into words on paper (and laboriously re-written if need be).

In the historical sense, arguably the first word processing *systems* were those of Gutenberg and Caxton, whose printing presses first opened the way to the vast proliferation of recorded human knowledge. Their development of moveable type made it possible to establish the vast platform of textual information on which the industrial and technological revolutions of succeeding centuries have been based.

The printing press can be credited with the fact that over 90 per cent of all scientists who ever lived were still alive in 1984, while at the same time all the world's major problems might be cured in a couple of years if even 10 per cent of the sum store of human knowledge could be made available in a single library in a universally understood language.

The typewriting machine, developed in the nineteenth century to meet the growing production needs of the paper factories which offices have become, was the next major word handling machine.

Surprisingly soon after the fairly widespread introduction of typing machines into offices, came what might be seen as the first word *re*-processor equipped with a 'memory' made up by holes punched in cards or on a pianola-type roll. Such machines were already in use in the 1890s in the United States for such applications as census recording. (The punched card for WP thus surprisingly pre-dates considerably its use in data processing, excluding production control of the Jacquard loom type.)

In the 1920s, cheap and effective WP machines based on punched-hole rolls were on offer for what is often regarded as the classic WP application – customizing standard letters. But perhaps the first genuinely flexible WP system was the Friden Flexowriter of the 1940s, merging at the printout stage streams of words punched in paper tape.

This was emulated in the early 1960s by typewriters with new, single-element print heads replacing the conventional type basket, and supported by magnetic tape memories in which words, paragraphs and even whole document sections could be stored, for subsequent editing and merging with new input or other stored material. These were succeeded (but probably never bettered) by the magnetic card typewriter and, in fairly quick succession, upgraded to flexible (floppy) magnetic disk memories.

Computer disks brought with them increasingly sophisticated control logic and an assortment of different displays on which text could be viewed for editing: single-line LED displays, six-line 'windows' onto text, 24-line and full-page cathode ray tubes.

All these options are still available, but this book homes in on the general configuration which came by the mid-1980s to represent what most users of the term understood by word processing – even on a personal computer.

This configuration consists of a microprocessor (or more often two or three of them) supported by substantial main memory (again on a microchip) and backed by sizeable disk memory (usually twin floppy drives, but increasingly involving at least one hard disk – see section 2). And again, by the mid 1980s, it was generally recognized that a word processing product without the facility to communicate (a) with others of its own kind, and (b) eventually with a whole host of other types of system and sub-system, would not last into the 1990s. So this book deals with advanced, screen-based systems having significant communications potential, and treats them consistently as the basic building-block for the office of the future.

But the potential user of WP should, however, also include in middle and long-term planning the rapidly developing lower echelons of microprocessor-supported electronic correcting typewriter. These are now cheaper in many cases than their electro-mechanical inferiors, and, if clustered together with a communicating interface to a more powerful WP system, can extend very far and wide the electronic text catchment area.

1.2 THE TECHNIQUES OF WP

Facilities and features of WP systems are described in considerable detail in section 3 of this book, but the basic aim of using WP remains simple: to eliminate all unnecessary effort at the keyboard. This is achieved partly by making it very quick and easy to see and correct typing errors, before anything is committed to paper.

But the essential strength of a WP system lies in its ability to store text for long periods and then to recall it for printing, at any time, in a virtually limitless variety of formats and combinations with newly input and/or other stored information. Nothing need be re-keyed once it is entered correctly and checked; any piece of text ever used in an organization can be stored and re-worked in a hundred ways. And the computer control needed to manage the very complex internal elements of a WP system produces multiple benefits at the user interface.

Difficult forms typing is a thing of the past – the machine takes care of forms control and formatting to 100 per cent levels of conformity with corporate style. Copy typing from audio dictation emerges from the depths of drudgery to become an attractive new form of author–typist interaction.

Properly applied, WP techniques make life much easier for direct and indirect users, substantially enhance the quantity, quality and uniformity of output. But, perhaps most importantly, they pave the way for progressive introduction of the integrated electronic information handling system for offices of the future.

2

Why word processing?

Before detailing the specific reasons why word processing is desirable for offices, it is perhaps convenient to address a much broader issue – why automate the office?

There are three principal answers to this question:

(1) to use computer power to make commercial and administrative information more readily available in a more easily understandable form;

(2) because investment in office equipment has historically run well below levels of investment in the agricultural and industrial revolutions preceding what might be called the information technology revolution; in manufacturing industry, shop-floor investment exceeds that in offices by factors of 25:1 and often higher. On the farm, the ratio has been at least 5:1 in favour of farming systems;

(3) computer costs continue to decline sharply in relation to the real costs of employing people; computers can save costs and enhance office productivity if properly applied. Costs directly attributable to office work now run well over 40 per cent of all overheads in most commercial enterprises.

2.1 WORD PROCESSING BENEFITS

WP delivers a number of specific financial and operational benefits in the office environment. It saves people costs wherever any text needs to be re-keyed using conventional equipment, and at the lower end of the WP equipment range – the electronic typewriter – machines are now actually substantially cheaper than their electromechanical predecessors.

For the direct end user, WP presents a wide range of improvements in working environment and throughput potential, chief among which are:

- typing speeds tend to be enhanced, typically by between 20 and 30 per cent for experienced keyboard users, much more for the part-time user
- increased speed of keying no longer means a corresponding decrease in literal accuracy
- presentation of documents in a uniform company style can be enforced without effort by a powerful layout control facility
- alterations are easily made, whether minor or major, and the drudgery of total re-typing of documents for relatively small changes is eliminated.

For the indirect user, too, there are many immediate advantages to having work done on a word processor rather than on a conventional typewriter. These include:

- an assurance that anything typed right at the first draft pass will stay unchanged; since as much as 20 per cent of the errors in a new draft may be introduced at the keying stage for that draft using conventional equipment, WP can very substantially cut the time an author needs to spend checking second and subsequent drafts.
- reduction of typing pressure on the skilled keyboard workers means that the author can spend longer thinking about contents
- stylistic or minor changes to a typed draft can be made with confidence by the author, without inundating the typist; larger sectional changes involving page-numbering and other upheavals with a text no longer mean large delays and frayed tempers
- in many instances, particularly those involving professionals using highly technical terminology, minor editing can be

carried out on drafts by the author, so that the typist does not need to be a qualified researcher in order to get the spelling right
– selection of secretarial personnel can be biassed more towards organizational and people-handling skills rather than keyboard artistry; a WP system means that even two-finger typists cannot be distinguished from those with years of touch typing experience.

2.2 THE BEST WAYS TO USE WP

Two very arbitrary, and erroneous views of the uses of word processing still appear to be widely held in the mid-1980s, despite a decade of successful usage of advanced WP systems. These views are that:

(1) WP is for standard text of the type used for mass mailing of personalized letters;
(2) the techniques of word processing are best applied only to one or two types of work.

The well-demonstrated fact is that, once any organization or individual can justify the use of WP systems for *any* application, they can and should be used for virtually all of them.

Among the most productive applications for which WP can be cost-effectively introduced are:

– iterative drafting of medium and large-sized documents, for the reasons cited above
– audio typing, in which there must inevitably be a second draft, since typists who can reproduce with 100 per cent accuracy the often indistinct and serially corrected audio input from dictators are rare; authors who feel no need to make changes once they see the spoken word in black and white print are even rarer
– updating of large reference and procedural manuals
– elimination of 80 per cent or more of the second keyboarding normally required in transferring typewritten text to typeset form
– filling in complex forms.

The list is by no means exhaustive, and must also obviously include the semi-standard and standard text assembly work with which WP has historically been associated.

Even typing addresses on envelopes (or sticky labels) can be time and cost-saving when associated with list processing logic in the WP system, able selectively to generate list of addresses and associate them with personalized detail in the text to be mailed.

It is probably still true that the best and quickest way to get out a three-paragraph memorandum from the Managing Director is for his secretary to type it on a machine which prints out directly, since

(a) three paragraphs is a small amount of text with low probability of literal errors, and easy to re-type quickly
(b) while a WP system would ensure 100 per cent accuracy at the first pass, and be slightly faster at the keyboard stage, it takes overall longer because of the need to set up a document at the start and then wait for it to be printed out at the finish.

However, if there is a slightest chance that a typing error will be made and/or that the MD will change his mind about a couple of words when he sees the text typed out, then it should be captured and stored electronically, on a machine able to store at least one A4 page of text at a time.

3

Technical background

Having established what word processing is, and the principal reasons why it may be applied, we should now look in some detail at *how* WP systems are put together, in hardware and software terms. This examination is directed principally towards the most powerful form of WP system, i.e. one dedicated to word processing as its primary function. However, as hardware for personal computers becomes steadily more powerful, and the nature of software for such highly intelligent terminals increasingly multi-functional, the more advanced personal systems – often termed 'professional' as opposed to 'home' computers – must be considered in the same light. Just as the demarcation line between dedicated and part-time WP is being rapidly eroded, so formerly drawn distinctions between WP and Data Processing (DP) become fuzzy and irrelevant.

The new breed of powerful, stand-alone microcomputer is increasingly seen as the desirable norm for all professionally used information-handling work-stations, taking on a multiplicity of functions matching that required by their users. At the same time, many home users of less powerful micros are achieving quite a lot on the text editing front. This does not mean that the specific art of WP is dead (as announced in dramatic tones by one or two misguided industry seers), but rather that it is now coming to be seen in its proper light, as central to all information processing activity and an integral part of the functionality of any cost-effective work-station of the 1980s.

Personal computers, in the generic sense, have become so important in the field of WP since 1980 that a special section (3.3) dealing with this development has been included here, after detailed consideration of the hardware and software features required for advanced, screen-based word processing (sections 3.1 and 3.2).

3.1 HARDWARE

A WP system consists of five basic hardware modules: central processing unit, display, keyboard, backing store and print device (see illustrations).

3.1.1 Processor

The central unit usually consists of one or more microprocessor chips supported by a main solid-state memory, also on microchips. (This memory is still sometimes referred to as 'core' memory, partly because of its central nature, but more directly because of the wire-wrapped magnetic cores from which such central memory used originally to be expensively assembled; hence the phrase 'core-resident', more frequently used still in connection with software modules which need to be always in main memory rather than on disk.)

The processor chip (typically from one of the three main suppliers: Intel, Motorola and Zilog) should handle 16 bits of information (eight bits to a byte, which can represent one character) at a time, rather than the eight commonly found in the first generation of powerful stand-alone WP systems and most PCs to date. Word processing is one of the most demanding of all applications in terms of constant demands on processor time and the control of multiple devices; it needs a big logic engine.

If response times and general efficiency are to be satisfactory, WP also requires a lot of program to be held constantly in main

(Reading clockwise from top left corner): Central processing unit with two magnetic tape drives and a VDT (visual display terminal) sitting on top; an ergonomic-design, pillar-mounted VDT sitting atop a hard-disk drive unit; medium-speed line printer; integral CRT (cathode ray tube)/ keyboard work-station; floppy disk unit for both eight- and five-inch disks; bracket-mounted ergonomic VDT; high-resolution CRT with associated palette and vectoring 'puck', for inputting graphics. (Courtesy Penta Systems UK)

>

memory. Word processors used commonly to be built around processor chips with 64K main memories, and several (e.g. DEC and WANG) managed quite well with only 32K, supported by floppy disks from and to which program elements were shunted into and out of the main memory. However, to give satisfactorily fast response times and handle a multiplicity of operations in simultaneity, a system needs *at least* a 16-bit processor and 128K main memory. Several WP systems now use 256K, 384K or even massive 512K main memories, and the WP application will certainly be one of those to derive most benefit from the new generation of 32-bit micros coming onto the hardware market.

The main reasons for WP's vast appetite for such power are simple:

- a competent WP program (without major add-on modules such as standard paragraphs and list processing, see section 3.2) will take up at least 200K of computer code, most of which needs to be in main memory most of the time; a fully capable package can easily require over 600K; many quite powerful commercial DP applications can run in well under 20 K of main memory
- user input demands are complex, particularly where, for example, a powerful facility provides real-time format control to assist non-professional keyboard users
- in strictly DP terms, advanced WP is not one application, but an agglomeration of what would normally be several, all requiring to be run in the same real time, e.g. searching text for pattern matches in the foreground, with background print device control and telecommunication to a remote terminal, etc.

In the early days of advanced WP (roughly 1975–80) much argument went on about whether WP requirements were best met using shared central processors, or by dedicating a processor to each terminal. At the time, both camps were right in different ways.

It *was* cheaper to deliver a given amount of processing power per work-station by sharing the logic of a shared mini. This also made it possible (a) to share backing store and print devices economically, (b) to establish communication in background mode between systems at a reasonable cost, and (c) to establish tight management control over the use of all system facilities.

Against the shared-logic approach it was argued that (d) if the central machine failed, all users were deprived of WP facilities, and (e) it was difficult to get into WP at a low starting price; shared systems typically cost upwards of £50,000 for only a handful of terminals.

Against stand-alones, it was argued that, while they were relatively inexpensive, and the failure of one machine involved only the users of that machine, (f) it was not easily or elegantly feasible to share expensive devices such as printers, (g) central management was impossible, and that (h) one word processor dedicated to one user achieved no staff savings at all.

As in most human dealings, there was a good deal of right and wrong on both sides; the error stemmed largely from organizational rather than technical considerations. Shared-logic WP, for example, proved much more effective in achieving staff savings because it was usually implemented in a typing pool situation, where enhancements in individual productivity of two or three to one could rapidly be reflected in pool staff reduction. With secretarial WP, it was not possible to reduce numbers unless a major (often politically fraught) reorganization of the way in which secretarial support was provided was undertaken.

Technically, a hybrid solution was in any case the obvious eventual answer: using cheap microprocessor power to achieve optimal performance at each user terminal while providing central management and device control functions on a network linking all terminals.

Over the 10 years since the advent of advanced WP, this has, in fact, been the evolutionary path, with increasingly powerful workstations increasingly making shared use of expensive and sophisticated central resources: file handlers, print device controllers and communications servers. Logic is thus distributed rather than shared, with all terminals enjoying the benefits once ascribed to both shared-logic and stand-alone configurations.

3.1.2 Displays

The traditional display unit for advanced WP is the cathode ray tube (CRT), similar to (but giving a higher quality image than) the home TV tube. As tube and keyboard are the main points at which the end user makes direct contact with the system, considerable thought must be given to the ergonomic design of both.

Perhaps the most important consideration with the screen is the *stability* of the displayed image, closely followed by the clarity of the characters shown. Bouncing, flickering images and hard-to-read characters will cause eyestrain, headaches and a general disinclination to use the terminal for anything but short periods of time. The lack of stability evident in many home TV images is simply not acceptable for office users. Care needs to be taken with protecting screens against accidental image distortion. For example, the motor of a printer sited too close to the screen can cause the image to waver and flicker due to disturbance of the magnetic field it causes.

Stability of image must also *not* be confused with durability. A high refresh rate of the displayed image, and a very low residual display time ('dwell') for the displayed characters is essential. A number of currently (1985) vended WP systems do not obey these rules, with the consequence that, for example, text being moved from one position to another trails clouds of moribund character images after it, like aircraft condensation trails, and generally disturbs user vision. The choice of a phosphor tube coating which allows an image to die abruptly once it is no longer being refreshed is essential. Also, CRTs eventually degrade and, particularly where users prefer a high-intensity display and/or a standard menu is routinely displayed when the system is not being used, ghostly characters gradually begin to appear permanently 'etched' on the screen, causing confusion with the sharper brighter transient ones. When this begins to happen, the CRT must be replaced.

Character legibility is determined by two factors:

(1) brightness: this is a highly subjective user consideration and *must* be individually controllable at each work-station
(2) shape: this is determined largely by the size of the matrix of dots in which the character is delineated on-screen; 16 dots high by 12 wide is an ideal size, 9 X 7 is *just* acceptable. At 6 X 5 (used by some early systems), eyestrain can result and many mistakes due to confusion of image: the number 5 is for example indistinguishable from the letter S.

It is also important to have a hardware-selectable set of options for displaying the cursor: the travelling point of reference which tells the end user where he is working on the screen. This can take several forms: underline, highlighting of a single character block in reverse video, or rectangular 'framing' of a character, or character space, with a thin line of light, any of these blinking or non-blinking. Many people find it difficult to work with blinking cursors (especially blinking underlines); others prefer blink mode for instant reference.

Much debate has gone on (and still does) as to display colours. Experiment and experience tend to indicate that the most restful combination is to have characters illuminated in gold or light orange on a dark brown or black background. The majority of screens, however, have so far used green on black. There is a school of thought which proposes black on white, as the natural emulator of print on paper. While such a display certainly gives the closest approach to the printed end product, the quality of such a display, from the user viewpoint, can be more vulnerable to reflected room light than green or orange on black/brown. It is also debatable whether, since an ultimate aim of the electronic office should be substantially to reduce the use of paper as a recording medium, too much attention should be devoted to emulation of the obsolescent.

The size of the display, in terms of apparent page area, has also occasioned considerable and continuing argument, with proponents of the black-on-white screen tending to form the nucleus of a large school demanding at least A4 equivalent (i.e. roughly 50 lines of text up to 100 characters wide). This cannot be achieved by standard CRT raster-scan techniques, in which a screenful of 25 lines of text by 80 characters is close to a standard. Vector-painting techniques (see Glosssary) or new technologies such as multiple arrays of liquid-crystal displays (LCDs) are needed to give this size of sheet. In terms of normal working, it has been found in practice that a text 'window' 16–25 lines deep by 60–80 characters wide is perfectly acceptable, *provided* that text can be 'scrolled' sideways out to at least 160 characters, or roughly two widths of A4 portrait/vertical mode (= A3 landscape/sideways) at conventional 10-pitch printing space, and *up or down* through the entire length of a document.

Scrolling motion should be steady in either direction, and may be seen implemented close to ideally in a number of terminals including, e.g. the DEC VT-100 used for large-system WP. Backward scrolling is an important facility not always provided on WP systems, due to constraints related to the control of screen-buffer linkages. If backward scrolling is not provided, it can be time-wasting and infuriating to have to return to the start of a document (or even the top of a page for that matter) to make an adjustment of something just entered and then rolled off the top of the screen.

To achieve a harmonious physical relationship with the end user, screens should be mounted in their cases at an angle of between approximately 13 and 17 degrees to the vertical; ideally, the case itself will be further adjustable both as to height above the keyboard and angle of orientation towards the user's face.

The screen surface should be matt, to avoid the worst effects of reflected glare from normal office lighting. Any screen should be installed as far away as possible from naked light sources, and never directly under a fluorescent tube or with the CRT axis parallel to the lighting strip.

3.1.3 Keyboards

WP keyboards are typically laid out with a central block of keys in the standard national typewriter pattern (QWERTY, as the top six left-hand keys, denominating the UK norm, AZERTY the French version, etc.), surrounded by lines and blocks of special function keys.

Ideally, each function key should have a clearly defined single function, and there should not be more than about 20 of them (see User Interface, section 3.2) plus a control cluster for the cursor). A North (up) South (down) East (right West (left) cruciform configuration of keys (see illustration), separated from the central cluster, has been found generally easier to use than separate movement command keys embedded in the main keyboard or a function-key cluster.

It has been found that incorporating delete keys for characters and words at the top left and/or right of the standard typewriter key cluster can accelerate the work of both professional typists, who notice instinctively when they have keyed a character wrong and can eliminate the error without breaking rhythm, and hunt-and-peck users, who can quickly delete whole words, in which they will frequently have typed characters out of sequence.

The national character layouts for keyboard, and especially QWERTY, are often popularly supposed to have been designed for ergonomic balance and to optimize typing speed. They were, in fact, designed to stop the type-bars (carrying the characters) in a conventional, basket-type manual typewriter from clashing if the typist keyed too fast. The clash problem was eliminated many years ago with single-element (golf-ball) typewriters and sustained accurate typing speeds close to 200 words per minute have been achieved (in competition) with electric machines using standard keyboards. To

Typical stand-alone work processing configuration – keyboard and screen, processor and disk drives (box under desktop), letter-quality daisy-wheel printer (foreground) (Courtesy Logica VTS)

>

logica VTS

improve speed and reduce manual fatigue, other layouts have been tried. These include a 'standard' American layout with a number of relatively small changes designed to accelerate typing speeds, and the Maltronic (see illustration), which effectively divides the keyboard in half, assigns different angles of attack to each finger, and fairly radically re-distributes character responsibilities between the two hands.

Neither these nor others have achieved widespread utilization as yet, probably due to the fact that, virtually by definition, the fastest keyboard users available are those best trained in the use of conventional layouts. They take a long time to convert to new layouts (typically 9–12 months) and appear instinctively still to be affected by their basic training on the conventional layout. Even with non-expert typists, the standard national layout seems almost subconciously to impress itself on the typing mind. In the early 1970s, for example, experiments using straight alphabetical keyboards (ABCDEF, etc., from the top left-hand corner) proved that, while these were acceptable for information retrieval in which only a few characters were keyed, it proved difficult to impossible for users to key longer character sequences for inputting text to a database.

Physically, a conventionally laid out keyboard should present a very low profile above a working surface at which the end user works, and a shallow angle of inclination. Skilled (i.e. touch-typing) keyboard users have also expressed a preference for a fairly wide plane surface at the bottom of the keys, on which to rest (even if only momentarily) the base of the thumbs.

The keys themselves should have sculpted tops, cushioning the finger-tips, and be spaced reasonably well apart as, for example, in a conventional IBM golfball-head typewriter.

It is important for professional conventional keyboard users that hardware design of electronic keyboards achieve something close to the natural resilience (i.e. bounce-back) and noise of the electromechanical keyboard, since it appears that these two factors constitute an important element of subconscious feedback to the typist for fast, balanced speed and accuracy of keying. For all users, it appears essential that they be able physically to detect the point at which a key-stroke is 'committed' i.e. transmitted to the system, usually after the key has travelled about two-thirds of the way to its stop-point. This will be an important point to bear in mind as other

The Maltronic keyboard. >

PCD
Maltron
BS DEL. BS
ACCEPT
PRINT
PAGE
RECALL
CODE
SPACE
CHAR
RPT
NEW LINE
WORD
PARA
LINE
SET
SAVE
PAGE
JOB
CODE
RPT
PARA
CHAR
WORD
FUNC TION
SHIFT LOCK
SHIFT
PCD

keyboard types become available, such as the pressure-sensitive pad, or more recent experimental devices such as a keyplate which deduces from disturbance of ultrasonic beams transmitted across its face which key position the user has touched. It is worth noting in this context that the second highly successful home computer launched by Clive Sinclair (the Spectrum) went back to using a conventional keyboard rather than the touch-sensitive pad of the ZX-81.

A desirable feature, often preventing considerable irritation, is to have a light-emitting diode (LED) embedded in the top of the shift key, giving a clearly visible warning to avoid typing a string of characters in upper-case, for example.

3.1.4 Backing store

Floppy disks ('diskettes') of the eight- and five-inch diameter variety, single or double-sided and holding data at various levels of density have come to be regarded as the standard backing store for advanced WP systems. While not as reliable or durable as hard disks, the drives they used were initially much cheaper, and so were the actual media.

Disadvantages of using floppies include the fact that they can wear out after a time, since the read/write head of the disk drive is in actual physical contact with the surface of a diskette, as opposed to floating a microscopic distance from it, as with a hard disk. People using floppies in office environments often have an uncomfortable habit of leaving them about in far from clean areas, and occasionally forgetting admonitions not to write on them with ballpoint pens (the resulting mechanical distortions are not very healthy for either the disk or the read head of the disk drive).

Typically, a floppy disk will hold the equivalent of 60–100 sheets of A4 paper, with about 40 lines of 70 characters each per page. Recently, one-megabyte disks holding up to four times this amount have been available.

Increasing use is being made in professional work-stations of inbuilt five or six-megabyte Winchester-technology hard disks, more for reliability and speed of access (about 10 times faster than the average floppy) than any urgent need for the larger amount of information on-line. The new small hard disks have dropped rapidly

Inserting a floppy disk into one of two disk drives. On this system, both drives can be used for recording or editing text, after one drive has been used for loading system software into main memory. (Courtesy Logica VTS)

>

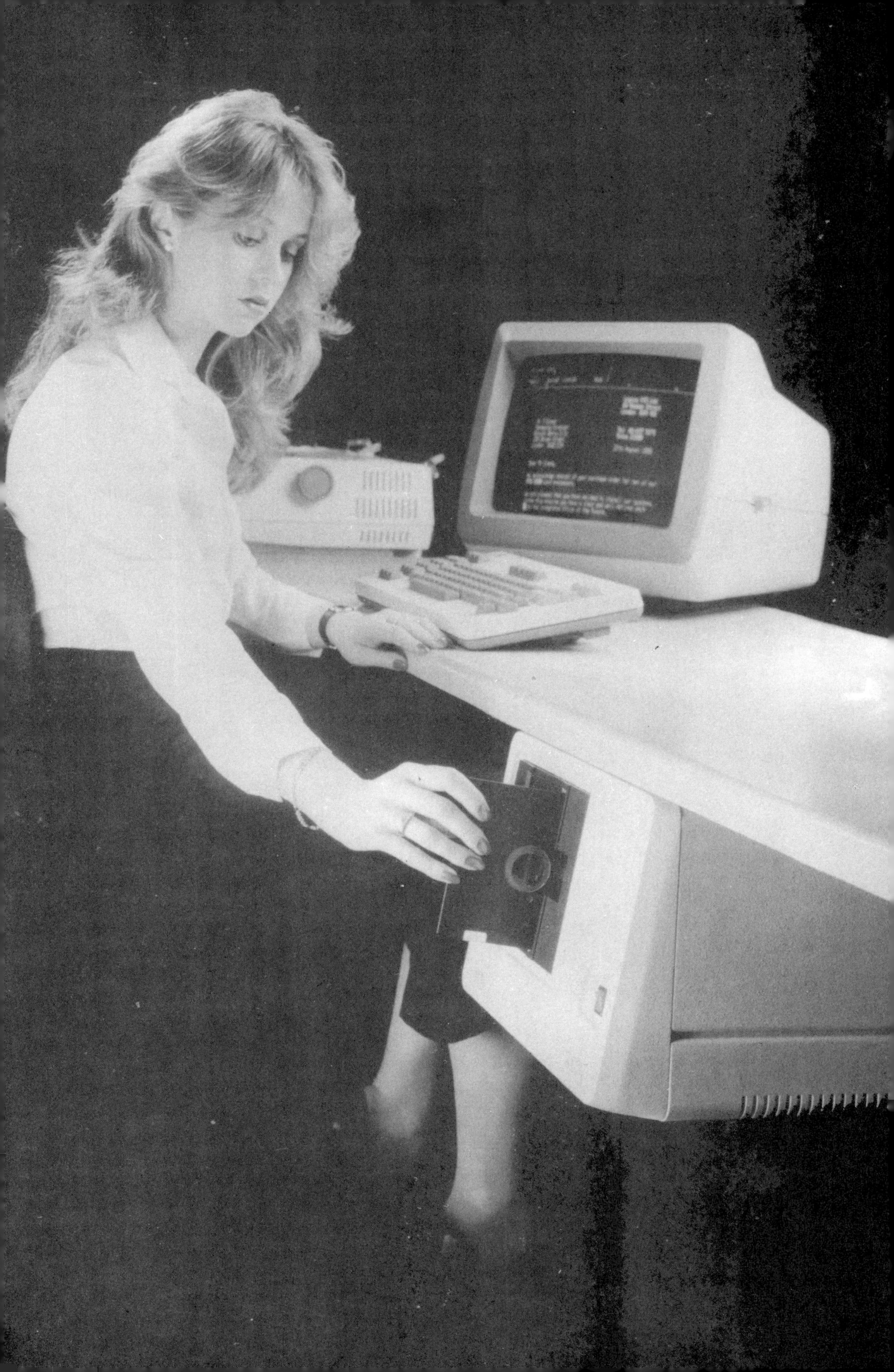

in price, making it as cheap (and easier to maintain) to fit one such drive as two one-megabyte floppies. However, most users need some kind of archival facility, and it is increasingly common practice to see a terminal fitted with a small hard disk drive and an archival floppy drive.

Small, three-inch diameter hard-disk cartridges holding about the same amount of information as a floppy, are being introduced and it seems likely – especially in view of their portability – that such storage devices may come into widespread use. Alternatives already being designed into highly portable systems for the mid-1980s include solid-state silicon ‘disks’, not needing a moveable drive, and RAM-chip mass storage cards to support intelligent transaction processing cards (see section 6). The possibility of being able to carry the essential elements of a WP system (CPU, backing store and communications controller) about in one’s wallet is anything but science fiction, for 1990.

At the big end of the backing store range are the very big, multiple-density hard disk systems. WP configurations have already been implemented using 800 megabytes (or something like 25 times the entire text of the Encyclopaedia Britannica) of disk storage.

High-density magnetic tapes, although obsolete for stand-alone WP systems for some 10 years, are still used in some of the larger office systems configurations for a reliable, cost-effective archival dumping mechanism to support fast-access disk storage.

For the second half of the 1980s, optical and laser technology disks, able to store three or four gigabytes (3,000 to 4,000 million characters) of text will be available for large configurations. One storage system capable of using 15 such disks rather like a jukebox is already in the pre-production prototype stage. Smaller relatives of these behemoths will undoubtedly be used as cheap and effective mass storage devices for smaller WP systems.

3.1.5 Print devices

Daisy-wheel printers (so-called because the print wheels resemble a daisy), usually with 96 characters per exchangeable wheel (as opposed to the 88 on a golf-ball head), were the staple equipment of the first generation of advanced WP systems. Thimble or shuttlecock-shaped

Daisy-wheel printer – delivers a letter-quality imprint at an effective printing speed of around 50 characters per second or an A4 page of text in about half a minute. (Courtesy Logica VTS) >

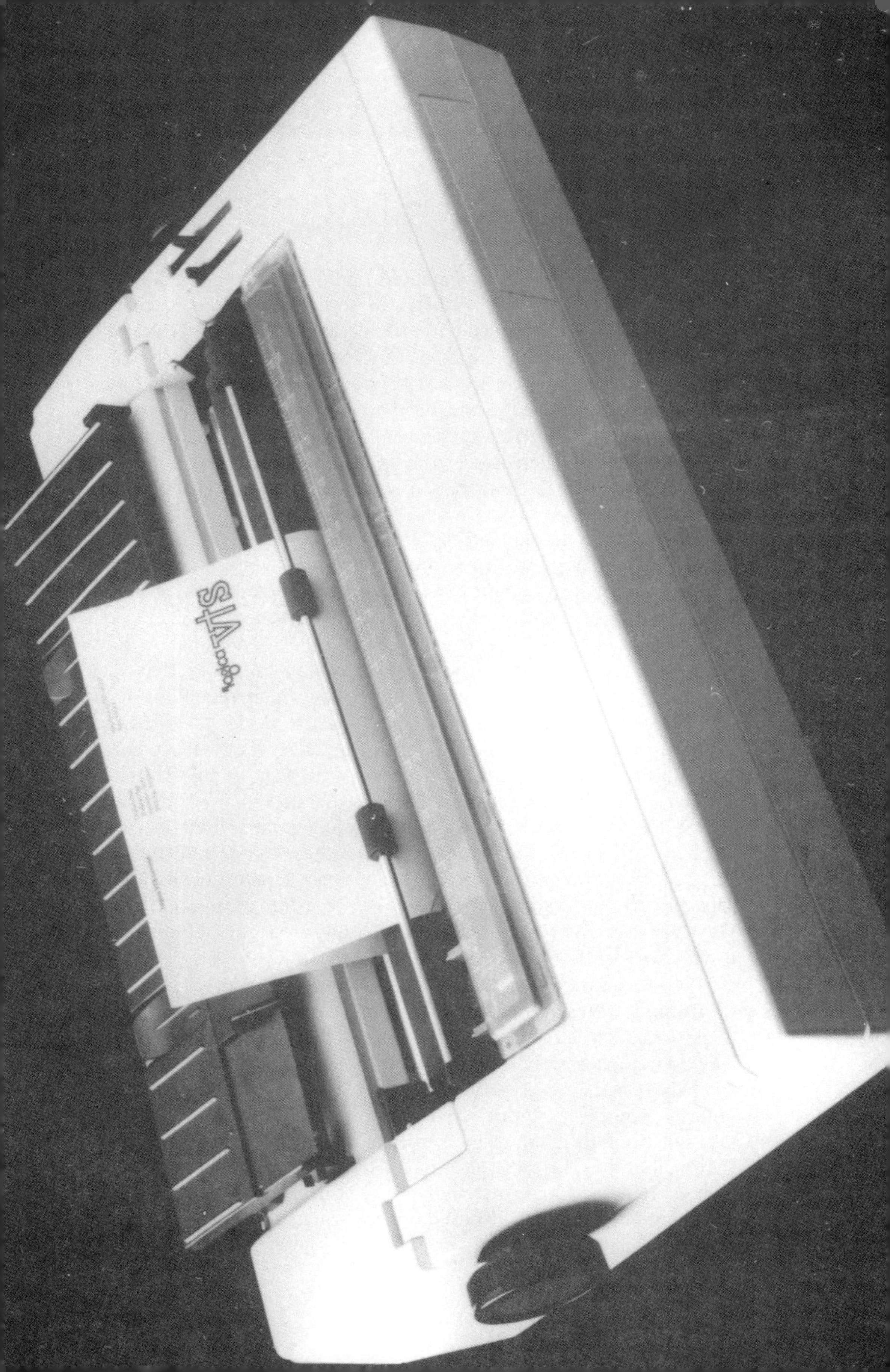

devices (such as on the NEC SpinWriter, for example) performed essentially the same job with a different hammer mechanism controlling the impact on paper.

The need to have more characters on line drove the development of impact, single-element printers in several directions, including the QUME twin-daisy device (either wheel addressable independently) with its very wide box, and concentric wheels whose two circles of characters (totalling as many as 192) are shifted up and down under the hammer by a logically controlled electromagnet. One supplier has also developed a single-daisy segment printer capable of producing (by building up characters from segments and overstriking two characters) over 300 characters to meet the full European Teletex fount.

Well before the end of the 1980s, convergence of printer and facsimile technology will have driven the more expensive end of the printer market into using hybrid devices capable of working in facsimile mode or being driven by streams of encoded characters. Several such devices are already on offer in 1984, and market pressures have been steadily driving the prices down. Given that such devices are based on established photocopier paper-handling technology, and can output text at anywhere from 15 to 100 times faster than conventional single-element printers, they will undoubtedly find a wide acceptance, particularly because of the flexibility of the typefounts they can reproduce (see Section 6).

At the lower end of the price range, thermal printers have developed very rapidly, at prices often less than 20 per cent those of the impact equivalent. Using tiny heated needle-matrices either with specially treated heat-reactive paper, or heat-transfer print ribbons, they can already give a very legible printed output, although not usually with quite the quality of a daisy wheel.

Needle-matrix impact printers, such as the Sanders, Facit and Printronix ranges, can also now deliver very high levels of print quality, almost indistinguishable from daisy-wheels and printed at least twice as fast, by using over-strike and back-stepping techniques with the matrix pins, to fill in spaces between the dots of the first imprint. Some very impressive results can be seen with full-colour printing using needle-matrix devices; like their daisy-wheel cousins, they will always have the additional advantage over black-and-white laser and thermal machines that they can print clear carbon copies, including blind carbons favoured by large banks for such applications as salary statement printing.

Ink-jet printers also look to have an interesting future for full-colour applications, and most of the early problems of unstable print image (slow-drying ink) and jet-clogging (fast-drying ink) appear to have been overcome.

3.1.6 Communications devices

Word processors, like other computer-supported devices working remotely, have historically needed modems (modulator-demodulators) to convert their digital output signals into analogue form for transmission over conventional telephone lines and then convert them back to digital forms at the other end. Modems are increasingly being built into the WP systems, and will, in the fairly near future, no longer be required in those countries whose telecommunications authorities provide fully digital packet-switched network services.

Universality of form and format are far from iminent (see section 4.6 on the importance of standards) and devices to facilitate interworking of like but not identically similar systems may be required late into the 1980s, if not beyond. Such devices are needed, for example, to:

- convert communications protocols (so that one machine knows how another will wish to converse with it)
- interpret formats (so that a receiving machine will know where and how its interlocutor wishes text to be presented)
- convert output (such as code-stripping for five-level telex, format imposition for teletex) to ensure that output from a WP system is rendered suitable for transmission over standard public-service lines.

Under the general heading of communications devices, local-area networks should also be mentioned, although they usually involve an assembly of devices and constitute more of a communications substrate. A whole book could be written about LANs, their connection to wide-area networks (WANs) and the developing argument between proponents of broadband and baseband implementation of LANs. But this book is concerned primarily with word processing and, to avoid devoting excessive space to another very large topic, it would perhaps be best simply to say that the LAN will play a very large and important role in the integrated electronic office.

The Shaftstall device which is used to convert floppy disks from various WP systems to be readable on various other types of system. (Courtesy Penta Systems UK)

>

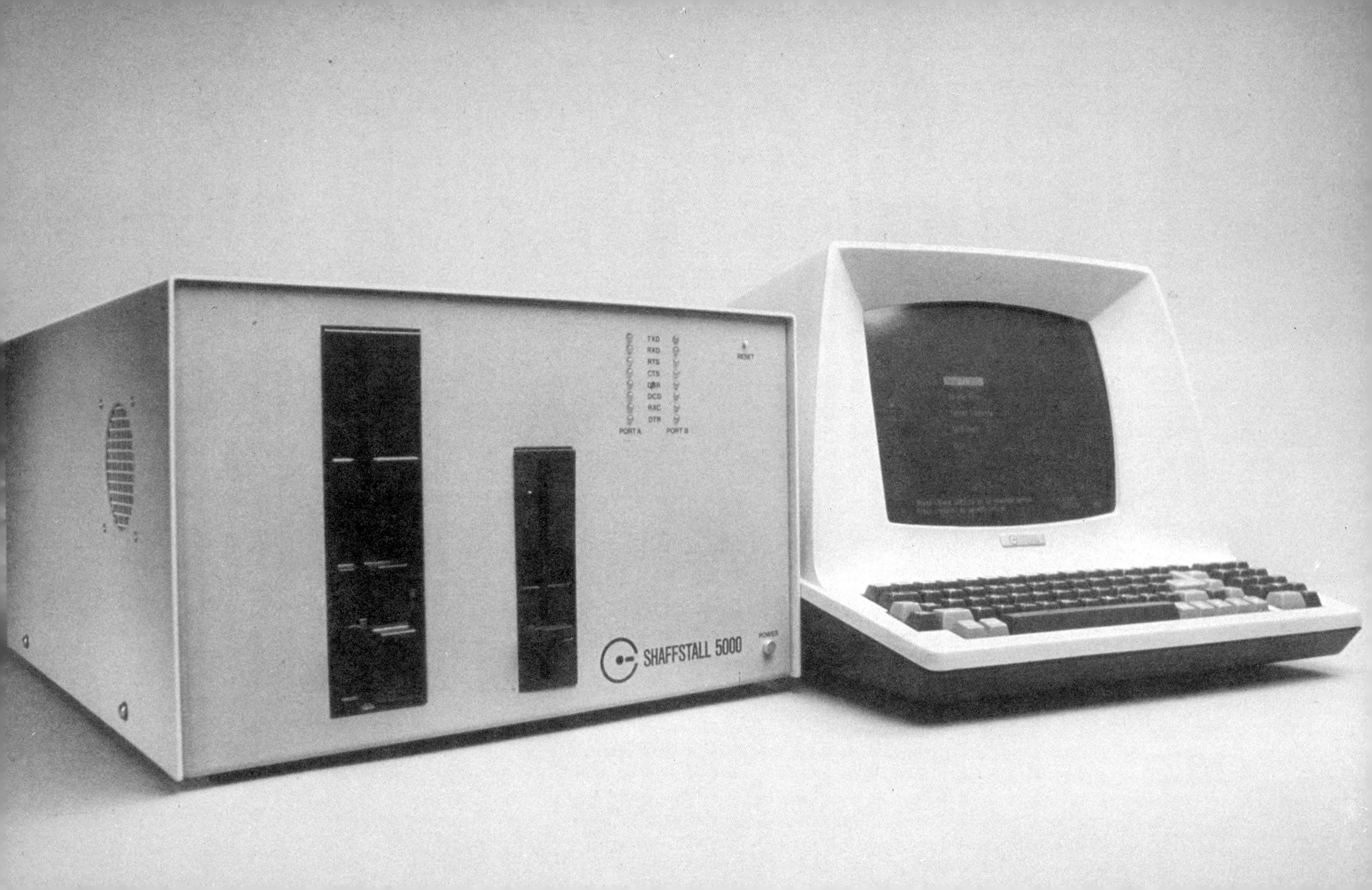
TXD
RXD
RTS
CTS
DCD
RXC
DTR
PORT A
PORT B
RESET
SHAFFSTALL 5000
POWER

LANs offer effectively device-transparent links for transmitting all forms of information (digitized facsimile and voice data as well as coded text and numbers) between widely differing types of work-station. What they do *not* do (although the misconception has been regrettably popular) is to provide the ultimate universal interface between unlike systems. What they *do* do rather well is provide an organized sharing of high-speed paths for diverse information streams.

Three basic types of LAN are offered:

– the Ring, UK versions of which are based on a system originally developed at Cambridge University and incorporating (in a closed ring) all the different types of available physical communications medium: twisted pair, coaxial and fibre-optic cable. Most implementations have been with the very economical twisted pair, down which Ring technology makes it possible to send data at effective transfer rates in excess of 4 million bits a second. Essentially, the Ring is a microprocessor controlled system of circulating 'data buckets' into which data is emptied and from which it is retrieved (or not) as the bucket stream passes a connected device. The system watches to make sure the bucket-loads arrive where they are sent, in the shape in which they are sent, and then forgets them. A major advantage claimed for Ring technology is that new work-stations can be added to or removed from the circuit without any pause to reconfigure the controlling software or hardware.

– the EtherNet: which was developed by Xerox, and has been adopted by other suppliers. With this approach, devices are connected in a tree-like structure to a high quality coaxial cable and must contend for use of the cable's transmission capability. Contention is detected by transmitting devices and is dealt with by a system of delayed re-transmission. The system provides less control information than a Ring.

– the 'big bus': a high-speed single line data highway linking a multiplicity of devices; this is a fairly standard offering for device connection from many suppliers.

Local-area network control box, and a reel of fibre-optic communications cable which can be used to transmit data at very high speeds between a multiplicity of devices connected on a ring-shaped network. Coaxial and/or twisted-pair copper cables may also be used with this system. (Courtesy Logica VTS)

>

polynet

3.2 SOFTWARE

The earlier sections of this book indicate clearly that, by 1990 at least, the choice of a specific manufacturer's hardware for use in offices will be a very minor consideration – it will be the quality of software run in that hardware which will count. Even with software, we are already seeing in the latest generation of powerful microcomputer some very strong trends towards standardization at the level of basic software, i.e. operating systems and utilities.

While there is also a clearly discernible long-term trend towards providing 'applications generators', or basic software tools enabling even quite atechnical end users to develop their own applications programs, it will probably be a long time before this happens with word processing.

As noted earlier, WP is a very demanding science. Text is unstructured and – if the richness of ethnic language and syntactical evolution are to survive – is likely to remain virtually unstructurable in many respects. By comparison, straightforward processing of numeric data having clearly established values and relationships, and structured into clearly defined fields, is child's play. For many years to come, therefore, it seems likely that serious users of WP, as opposed to those needing perhaps only a simple text editor, will continue to draw on, but enhance, the established designs and hard-learned lessons of previous designers.

One of the harder of these lessons learned in the late 1970s was that it can cost something between three and four million pounds to develop from scratch a competent word processing package, ruggedize it and launch it as a product, *before* the first pound of sales revenue comes in. One of the more disappointing features of the early 1980s is the extent to which systems suppliers have still failed to learn this lesson, and continue assiduously to re-invent the wheel, wondering why the end product is usually inferior to its supposedly obsolescent predecessors and costs twice as much to develop. Another is that most suppliers of WP packages and bundled systems for the mid 1980s still saw functional design aimed at the needs of fully trained computer specialists rather than providing simple utilities for sophisticated text handlers.

3.2.1 Simple user interface

The essence of success with WP, or any office system for that matter, is the ease with which the end user of that system can get to grips with its facilities. This means designing a simple interface between man and machine, adapting the machine to what its user needs done, rather than seeing how far he or she can be adapted to fit in with what the machine is good at doing. Ideally, the system will also provide several levels of interface: simplistic for the neophyte or perennially casual user, cutting corners for the more advanced user, and enabling full-time users to design personalized facilities around their own needs.

Simplicity of user interface has a number of implications, including the following:

- system usage will probably need to be menu-driven at the lowest level, i.e. inexperienced users should have very direct guidance by system displays as to what the first and all succeeding steps should be
- formatting of output must be very heavily system-controlled for the non-specialist end user, making it possible, for example, for a two-finger typist to output a document perfectly presented in corporate style, albeit perhaps marginally slower than a professional touch-typist. Forms can be designed and changed by supervisory staff, in the classic Organization and Methods departmental tradition; once entered into system software they need never be touched by user hand
- system-generated responses and advisory messages should be in clear ethnic English and wholly semantic. Vague phrases of broad application such as the notorious 'illegal command' must be replaced by more specific explanatory notes such as, for example, 'system cannot be closed while printing is in progress', or a clearly understandable abbreviation thereof
- a very powerful HELP facility, invoked by a single keystroke should be provided for all levels of user, to get them swiftly out of trouble and (ideally) indicate where they went wrong this time
- minimal mnemonics users: should not be asked to remember, or even have to look up, long tables of character sequences in order to execute simple commands. All basic commands should be clearly indicated on individual keytops; ideally no key should have more than one command value.
- users should not be aware of having to exit from one application program (say, editing) to enter another (say, printing or communication); all the applications useable at the termi-

nal should be executable in what appears to the end user to be the same mode. Ideally, the user should be able to stop editing, switch to communications, over to printing and back again to editing without ever having had formally to terminate and store work done in any of those modes, simply by keying one 'interrupt button'

– the system should generate automatic reminders to users to close down their system in a tidy manner, e.g. taking archival copies if necessary, removing disks from drives.

For more advanced users, the user-friendly menu approach taken by the most commercially successful WP system suppliers (e.g. WANG), can be irritating. Once they know their way round the basic facilities, users need simple short-cuts so that they can get straight into what they want to do instead of taking a guided tour of sequential manus. Providing these short-cuts is simple.

For the full-time, professional user, system friendliness needs to go a stage further, allowing him/her to custom-build basic new facilities, or high-speed short-cuts, amounting to quite powerful sub-routines in programming. This should emphatically *not* be done by allowing these end users to tinker with basic system software or even the supplied applications code. They should be given the facility to assemble/concatenate (chain together) instructions and execute them with a single simple command to form personalized sub-programs composed of absolutely standard sub-elements. This is done, for example, with use of GOLD key routines in Digital Equipment Corporation (DEC) based systems, or with the GLOSSARY facility in WANG Office Information Systems.

3.2.2 Key editing features

Well-trained demonstrators will make any WP system look to the prospective purchaser as though it has 95 per cent commonality with the editing package of any other system, plus a few distinctive bells and whistles. This is far from the case, and many of the 120-plus WP systems on offer in Europe in the mid-1980s are, in fact, missing some of the most basic requirements for successful editing. While all systems will permit the entry, deletion and movement of characters, words and phrases, that is about as far as commonality really goes; it is also true to a large extent of most basic electronic typewriters.

Key features which will distinguish a truly competent, user-oriented word processor from a simple text editor include the following.

- the system should be normally locked in text entry mode with all deletion explicit (rather than, for example, by over-typing); this avoids the need specifically to enter insert mode when adding text, and the danger of inadvertently deleting existing text
- single-key insertion of margins and tabs in a displayed tab-rack, with single moving elimination of tabs, and automatic insertion of a tab at the point from which a margin indicator is moved; preservation of all margins and tabs as set when the document is stored/retrieved. It must be possible for tabs to be set left of the left margin
- text should automatically 'wrap round' to the next line during continuous typing, so that no word is broken at the end of a line. The end user must be able to insert 'hard' (i.e. mandatory) carriage returns, e.g. at the end of paragraph or desired short lines.
- erase character (deleting previous character typed, for speed of correction during fast keying) and erase word (deleting from anywhere in the word or backwards from one character space ahead of it) keys, ideally located at the corner(s) of the central QWERTY alpha-character block
- single-key text close-up feature, limited by paragraph markers or blank lines, to re-format affected text within established margins, following insertion or deletion of characters, words or larger segments of text
- distinction between *blocks* of text and *strings* of characters. The former may be moved intact, with all their format controls, and placed elsewhere in text exactly the same shape as they were in their former habitat. The latter may be inserted anywhere and re-formatted with existing text. The distinction is also useful when deleting larger segments of text
- facility to move large blocks of text within a document or into another one, or chain together blocks or strings selected from various parts of a document and move them
- distinction between *copying* blocks or strings of text and *moving* them. In the former case, they can be reproduced elsewhere but leave the original intact; in the latter case,

they are cleared from their present position and moved elsewhere. Blocks and strings should be stored on disk as small jobs when being moved, and identified with short (say, three-letter codes) to avoid the possibility of losing them if the system should crash (most systems store text in transit in volatile main memory) or confusion when retrieving multiple blocks or strings. (N.B. a powerful block/string purge command should ideally accompany this as a housekeeping facility, otherwise a small disk can get very rapidly overloaded – see 3.2.9)

– table/columnar mode allowing the convenient manipulation of tabular material. This should prevent the (spectacularly awful) effects of ruining neatly serried ranks of typed figures by injudicious use of a standard text close-up feature. It should also provide such facilities as decimal point alignment of figures within columns, and tabbing down and back within columns (a great saver of typist effort). Ideally, this feature will also be associated with a simple mathematical calculation package adding down and across columns with cross-casting/verification of totals

– vertical line facility, ideally allowing continuous drawing of a vertical line by holding down a single key; this should be supported for printing purposes by an automatic 'corner-squaring' function to align vertical lines neatly with their horizontal partners, when drawing boxes, etc.

– all character, cursor control, insert and delete keys should be 'typamatic', i.e. repeat their function, when deliberately held down. Holding down cursor directional control keys should ideally accelerate cursor travel

– insert and delete line functions should be mandatory

– provision of a 'third shift', allowing typing of subscript or superscript (half a line up, half a line down, e.g. for chemical notation) and/or foreign characters or accents, is highly desirable

– the user should be able to specify 'hard' (i.e. required) hyphens (e.g. in semi-illiterate) and have the option to command the system to insert 'soft' (i.e. discretionary) hyphens at the ends of lines, to achieve a better right justification of text if desired. The system should automatically strip out soft hyphens when any editing of a paragraph containing them is carried out.

3.2.3 Forms design

The system should contain a powerful forms design facility, enabling supervisory staff to design standard forms to be used by all end users. Users can be kept updated by periodic issue of new forms software disks, in the case of stand-alone units, more directly by addressing the storage devices of all terminals hooked to a network, or simply pulling down forms at will over the network from a shared forms store.

The twin aims of all forms design software should be

- to cut down heavily on the excessive number and variety of forms used in any organization
- to ensure that users are not merely guided towards correct presentation, but positively prevented from presenting their material any other way, unless they create their own special form for an approved special purpose.

The features required of a powerful forms design facility will include:

- minimal keystroke (e.g. A5 + ACTION) summoning by end user of a selection of standard paper sizes in portrait (vertical) and landscape (horizontal) mode (A4, A5, and possibly A3 portrait usually suffice for most purposes). A4 (portrait) should probably be set as a default option on menu displays so that a single keystroke will bring up this most commonly used of formats
- complex forms (e.g. purchase orders) may be designed and displayed on-screen, operating for the end user in much the same way as a conventional DP format, i.e. tabbing quickly between fields where text must be entered.
- a facility to display text and outlines which will not be printed, for use with pre-printed proformas as a guide to the end user as to what his/her document will look like when printed
- a similar facility to display and print mandatorily text which cannot be edited out by the end user (e.g. required phraseology for insurance claim letters, etc.)
- a facility to store with its format semi-standard text which can be edited by the end user, or a mixture of such text and mandatory verbiage
- the ability to handle multi-part forms where several significantly different page layouts may be incorporated as part of a single document

- a design facility to enable the supervisor clearly to identify where he/she is in the design, as between free, partly changeable and non-changeable pre-set text, and to specify automatic printout or print suppression of certain parts of what is displayed
- the ability to define address boxes, and identify these logically to the list processing package (see section 3.2.6)
- a facility taking the cursor immediately to the point at which a user should start typing
- a re-design facility to produce multiple variants of a given form without starting from scratch
- the option to suppress printing of system-generated document reference numbers
- a facility to identify first pages separately from continuation pages of a document
- the facility to summon a copy of any standard form by keying a simple, supervisor-defined character sequence (e.g. INVOX for Invoice)
- the ability to turn any document types on the system into a standard form.

3.2.4 Document orientation

It is *essential* that the design of a WP system be wholly document oriented, and not geared simply to the generation and editing of pages, paragraphs or even lines of text.

This has a number of major implications for software design, including:

- all re-formatting commands must be capable of being applied, if required, across the entire contents of the document typed (e.g. set within narrower or expanded margins)
- search facilities must be global and not page restricted (as they are with some early WP systems); it must be possible to search through a whole document for all occurrences of a given character sequence, whether in upper or lower case or a mixture of the two. It must also be possible to carry out an accelerated search by system-generated page number
- the system should automatically number pages, and carry out a re-numbering exercise if necessary after heavy deletion and/or insertion exercises. (N.B. Manual override of the automatic

numbering system should also be allowed, to cater for the introduction of extra pages of graphics, etc., generated outside the WP system)

- a powerful facility must be provided to pull together in one large job (at least for printout and page numbering purposes) a number of sections of a document which have been created as individual jobs in the system. Transfer of part or whole of a document to be incorporated into or concatenated with another must likewise be easily achievable
- spacing between lines should be capable of being altered for a whole document, or selectively within the document.
- document integrity and unique identity must be preserved in communication to other systems.

3.2.5 Storage and retrieval

It is a basic requirement of any WP system that the retrieval reference for any document *must* be unique when created and kept that way. This may be achieved either by

- having all retrieval references generated by the system, with a sequential numbering check to prevent duplication, even after deletion of a document from system storage
- leaving end users free to invent their own retrieval reference, subject to a swift directory check by the system to ensure such a reference does not already exist
- a mixture of system and user-generated references.

For any configuration in which WP systems are to communicate between each other, it is *essential* that each work-station tied to a network add its own unique originating-system identifier to the retrieval reference. Assuming the systems to be similar or identical, they will otherwise probably generate many identical references; human users will always manage to do so.

While generation of unique references takes care of short-term chronological filing, assuming that either (a) all system references are printed on the documents to which they refer and/or (b) the system has an easy-reference directory containing adequate user-defined identity parameters (which it should), for the longer term, users will need to move more towards wider, perhaps topic-oriented retrieval of information across much larger file structures; the 'electronic filing cabinet', providing an office-oriented sub-set of the larger systems described in another book in this series (E. N. Teskey, *Principles of Text Processing*, Ellis Horwood, 1982).

The first requirement will be to identify and retrieve a document or section of one, possibly by only one or two search parameters out of a dozen largely forgotten: e.g. sent *about three weeks ago* to somebody *Smith*, about *turtle soup* (that should find it fairly quickly in a good free text system). This will replace the invaluable paper mess in the executive bottom drawer, but the longer-term need is for fully structured retrieval not only from text generated in-house, but all related material coming from the outside world, in whatever form or format.

3.2.6 Heavy text manipulation

Word processing techniques are perhaps used at their most powerful when assembling, manipulating and re-formatting documents from standard and semi-standard text held in store, and then integrating it with fresh input.

The classic WP application is the personalized standard letter, for which mechanical typewriters driven by punched cards and pianola-type rolls were used as far back as the 1920s. Customer names and addresses were filled in by manual keyboard operation and the typist then let the paper-stored text do its work. In exactly the same way, word processors can be used for mass generation of ostensibly individually typed documents – the 'standard letter' application.

In one area of heavy text processing – list processing – the more powerful word processing systems overlap very considerably with (and in some cases take over from) data processing systems. One widely used development of this application, combined with standard letters, is the dunning letter, with which defaulting debtors can be pursued by a series of increasingly demanding letters, each with the latest state of debit account interwoven with the words. The use of WP is said to be far more effective than conventional computer-generated or pre-printed warning notes; debtors apparently feel that any organization taking the trouble to type individual messages is getting serious about suing them, so they tend to pay up.

Integration of quite extensive and complex background material, often drawn down from a mainframe computer's files, can be achieved on word processors with suitable batch file transfer interfaces to the main computer.

An even more effort-saving application is seen with semi-automatic generation of contractual documents from stored standard paragraphs or document sections. This has a distinct advantage over conventional typing of such material in that (a) logical include or exclude commands can be associated with certain text elements (e.g. if paragraph 51 is used, 52b must be excluded) and (b) the final output is immediately letter-perfect. a basic requirement for all legal documentation, of which manual corrections are taboo.

Many governmental (and not a few commercial) organizations also have heavy text re-formatting requirements, needing to present extracts from documentation in different ways, or in many cases simply to print out exactly the same text in a different typeface or layout. WP is ideal for this, especially when the system can take care of re-formatting needed, for example, when switching from 10 to 12 or 15 pitch typefaces in printing a large document.

One large British manufacturing concern maintains a very sophisticated text processing system which holds in constantly updated standard paragraphs the manuals for its various large mechanical products, in 21 different ethnic languages. Even without knowledge of the foreign language, a system operator can, for example, automatically generate a new service manual in Spanish, by keying in the same paragraph numbers as for the English version. The Spanish text will emerge, some 40 per cent longer (the language is somewhat more circumlocutory than English!) but perfectly re-paginated and formatted – and even leaving room for the same standard part drawings and illustrations.

Another heavy piece of manipulation previously performed on large mainframe and mini-computers is alphanumeric sorting of large lists. A classic application is sorting office telephone directories into alphabetical user order, then by department and sometimes further, by number.

3.2.7 Print control

Given that the principal end product of word processing is (or will be for at least the next few years) text printed on paper, powerful print control is crucial to the art. Unfortunately, many system suppliers seem to have become somewhat prematurely fascinated with the art of manipulating text in purely electronic form and tended to ignore the more mundane business of actually getting the words out on paper. Interestingly, this tendency is quite often found in most pronounced form where the supplier approaches WP from the DP man's point of view, rarely where the supplier looks at it from the typist and author standpoint.

It is *essential* for a good WP system that printing be able to take place in background mode, i.e. carry on while the user is editing another document on-screen and/or ideally while text is being received from or communicated to another terminal, if desired. Most personal computers in use in the mid-1980s and (quite surprisingly) several dedicated word processing systems were not able to achieve this. This requirement relates directly to the operating system used, which must be of the concurrent run-time type, allowing several applications to be run in the background while one occupies the foreground, all in the same real time.

In terms of application package design, the following are important requirements for a good WP system:

- print queue: it must be possible to queue several items to one printer or, in the case of shared-resource/networking systems, to a variety of print devices (N.B. in the latter case, this queueing requirement may be met by the software of a print server – a microcomputer sub-system dedicated to controlling a multiplicity of print devices). It must be possible for the queue to be re-ordered by the end user and (most importantly) for items to be removed from it at short notice (e.g. when users change their mind)
- the print control module of a WP system must be able to take full advantage of the range of functions offered by any print device, including managing the often quite extensive control logic found in even electro-mechanical printers
- users should be able to specify the printing of any single page of a document, a range of pages within the document, or the whole document; too many systems still demand the reprinting of a whole document in order to reprint just one or two altered pages.
- ideally printer directives should be associated with a separately grouped set of keys, and messages regarding print status should be displayed on-screen to the end user
- to facilitate remote printing and transfer to other systems, a print store display should automatically record the number of pages in a document and type of form to be used. This information must be transferred with the document when it is communicated.

- the print module should be able to take advantage of the logical controls offered by twin-sheet hopper feeders, so that header sheets may be inserted ahead of continuation pages, etc. by addressing separately the feed mechanisms for the two hoppers
- the system should be able to work in single-sheet mode or using continuous stationery, with suitably adjusted paper throws at page-end for various sizes of paper if continuous stationery is used
- it must be possible to stop printing in mid-course and restart (a) from the point where printing was stopped, (b) from the top of the page, (c) from the top of any specified page, (d) from the beginning of the document
- end-of-ribbon and ribbon break advisory messages must be displayed on the screen and the printer automatically stopped for printers using ribbons; ink or toner supply failure should similarly be notified for ink-jet and laser printers. It is most important that this information be communicated back to a sending terminal in the event of remote printing
- paper-out warnings, and advice of continuous stationery failures must be communicated where hopper feeders and/or continuous stationery are being used, *especially* when the drive is remote
- all print devices must communicate 'ready-to-print' advisories back to the sending system; where printing is remote, block check mechanisms to detect and eradicate possible data corruption in transmission must also be provided
- it must be possible to change between-line spacings up or down at printout by direct command to the printer, as an alternative to doing this with the text in electronic form
- at least 10, 12 and 15 pitch horizontal spacing must be selectable on the output device
- in the event of system failure, any document in the print queue or in process of being printed must be protected against corruption/loss and retrievable from disk on re-starting the system
- any user attempt to shut down the system while printing is in progress, or to remove a disk from which printout is being made, must be blocked.

3.2.8 Background communications

Apart from the print control communications requirements outlined in section 3.2.7 for remote working of print devices, interchanges between WP work-stations must take place in background mode.

For exchange of messages and documents, an 'electronic in-tray' facility, of the kind required for effective electronic mail (q.v.), must be provided. This should:

- ensure that incoming documents are assigned local retrieval cross-references, if necessary, and properly stored
- acknowledge receipt to the sending system
- automatically request repeats of corrupt or dubious blocks of data received
- advise the work-station user immediately of any urgent messages, using the status line of his display, and periodically advise him if he has received any mail at all
- build and maintain a directory of all mail received, for regular inspection.

3.2.9 Housekeeping/system management

Good housekeeping and orderly management of system facilities and devices are important to the success of any size of WP installation, whether the choice be stand-alone work stations, a highly centralized configuration or a distributed network of intelligent terminals. In the last two cases, they can even be crucial to survival and normal running, let alone success.

Housekeeping and management facilities which must be built into any professional WP system include:

- protection against data loss in the event of system failure, limiting losses to not more than one screenful of newly created information at most; ideally the system will write newly entered data from buffer store to disk in completed blocks of 256 characters, so that maximum potential loss will be less than this (about four lines of text)
- directory of contents, to be viewed either on a work-station screen, or printed out, preferably both. This should contain at least the following details about every document (except those classified as private):

  retrieval code
  author
  title/topic

date first entered
date last used
expiry date (author-specified)

- purging facility, to remove from storage outdated materials and re-format cleared areas to take on new material; this should allow deletion of

  specific documents
  nominated groups of documents
  all documents past expiry date
- archival copying facility
- copying mechanisms to:

  take backup copies of disks
  copy jobs within the same disk to other disks

- recover all uncorrupted jobs in the case of data corruption or possible write-head failure of a disk drive
- warn end users when disks are 75 per cent and 90 per cent full; prevent entry of more information after disks are 98 per cent full
- initialize/format new disks
- supervise read-before-write checks on disk sectors, to avoid the quite frequent problem of data corruption due to attempts to write data to disk sectors which are supposedly blank but actually contain residual characters from earlier occupancy.

In order to facilitate sizing and justification for future expansion of the system, it will also be of considerable value for the housekeeping module to gather and report on statistical information relating to:

- system activity: CPU loadings
  disk re-tries
  print queue lengths
  search execution times
- work-station stats: original keystrokes
  text amounts retrieved
  printer output

3.3 WP AND PERSONAL COMPUTERS

Many personal computers now offer WP packages but, until very recently, the limitations of their main memory (typically 64K maximum), and their ability to run only one application at a time, severely constrained the design, and consequently capability of these machines.

During 1984, the hardware scene changed rapidly, with 'professional' personal computers (i.e. those used by managers and professionals rather than hobbyists or home users) having up to 512K main memories, often several magabytes of disk storage, and the consequent ability to use quite sophisticated WP packages.

The parallel development of concurrent run-time operating systems for PCs, such as concurrent CP/M, allowing, for example, editing, printing and telecommunication to take place in the same real time, has also cleared the way for complete emulation of the professional word processor by the increasingly indistinguishable PC. Indeed, towards the upper end of the professional micro market there are now a number of multi-purpose hardware offerings able to run variants of advanced WP software packages offered in a more dedicated form by the same supplier, or a variety of software packages for DP on a machine chiefly used for WP. Examples include IBM DisplayWriter and PC, the WangWriter and PC, and the Logica 2200/Vitesse WP/PC combinations.

This section looks at some of the distinctive features of WP for personal computers, as regards user needs, system hardware and software.

3.3.1 User needs

The range of user needs for text editing facilities on a personal computer, which is intended to be used for several purposes, is considerable.

At the bottom end of the scale is a need for a very simple text editor, possibly operating on only a single line at a time, to prepare and alter programs and program documentation. Home users whose PC configuration includes a printer with a reasonable-quality typeface will also often use it for writing short notes or more advanced documentation, at which point they start to need a format control facility to handle at least a full page at a time. A fair number of authors, of popular fiction as well as professional textbooks, now use word processing packages on home computers. Their needs move still further up the scale, requiring a system which can, for example, allow them to move blocks or strings of text within an entire document, and to send a multi-page document for printing, instead of operating one page at a time, as with simpler units.

vitesse
reset

At the top end of the range comes the fully 'professional' user of the PC for multiple applications, often with a need to produce and manipulate to a significant extent quite heavy text, typically documents of 40–60 pages. He or she needs a fully typist-compatible form of advanced WP, often with alphanumeric sorting and facilities for plagiarism (i.e. transferring selected portions of one or more already existing documents into a new document being created).

Such exponents of what is increasingly known as 'End User Computing' (EUC for short) will often wish to edit bulk text entered by professional typists. On the other hand, it is already quite common practice in some organizations for these keyboard specialists to be asked to carry out for their authors/editors simple DP functions (typically spread-sheet calculations and similar work) in between their typing activities. Such a mixture of professionalisms demands not only a highly flexible suite of software packages, but also a largely user-transparent complexity of WP software equal to that of the most advanced dedicated systems.

3.3.2 Hardware considerations

The first generation of personal microcomputer hardware did not lend itself over-well to advanced WP, for three principal reasons: processor power, configuration cost and suitable software. As we have seen earlier in this chapter, a competent WP vehicle needs quite a big engine to pull it along, and eight-bit 16K, 32K or even 64K processors are not quite in the right category.

The arrival of economically priced, second-generation 16-bit 128K or even 256 K machines on the market, and the prospect of cheap 32-bit machines soon to come, has changed the power consideration quite dramatically.

The overall cost of building a full WP-compatible configuration, with two disk units and a high-quality print device (the latter being usually the highest priced module), would until very recently tend to arrive at a figure beyond the range of most non-professional users and not all that different from a completely packaged, WP-dedicated system. Many early PCs, for example, worked on a basic

Professional work-station. A personal computer for use by managers, technicians and other professional users. The hardware used is virtually identical with that of the WP systems shown in other illustrations, but WP is just one of many information processing packages which this < *machine handles. (Courtesy Logica VTS).*

screen display only 40 characters wide. This meant having to buy an 80-character line expander board or else limiting text lines in documents to four or five words (not very acceptable in communication with others, apart from short notes) or introducing design and operating complexities by working in half-lines, to be linked together at printout. Early *home* PCs also relied heavily (for price reasons mainly, but in some cases temporary availability, due to sheer weight of demand from buyers) on tape recorders for program and file storage, with all the problems and delays of serial access to stored data which this implied. From the early 1980s onward, however, random-access floppy disks at an increasingly reasonable price have been an increasingly attractive option for even the smaller machines.

With the advent of the middle 1980s, the cost and architectural differentials between WP and multi-purpose *professional* PC configuration have been reduced to triviality, and it is increasingly a matter of choosing the system with the right blend of multifunctionality.

3.3.3 Software packages

While many simple DP programs can be written, or basic packages extensively adapted, by the PC user, advanced WP is simply too complex and large a task for this to be undertaken.

The package, either bundled in with a total system design (and price) or as a separate module runnable on several hardware types and configuration, is therefore the preferred answer. This is especially true since – as we have seen earlier in this chapter – WP facilities may be enhanced, but the needs they meet are fairly constant and generally accepted.

WP package design was a problem with the earlier generation of single-application eight-bit machines, in which the system could, for example, only handle text entry and editing *or* printing at the same time. Text handling also typically required extensive use of complex command codes, and packages were in consequence generally difficult to use, except for those people already having some skills in data processing techniques.

Against this background, one package, WORDSTAR, became preeminent in the PC world. For a fairly low price (typically about £300, but depending on the precise system for which it was configured) this package delivered quite powerful WP functions and, with an associated sorting package for mailshots (MAILMERGE) provided a full basic WP repertoire.

Nonetheless, packages designed for micros only able to run one application at a time were inherently less attractive than dedicated WP systems which, in their second and third generations, could handle text entry and editing in foreground mode, while carrying out printing and/or communication of other work at the same time in background mode.

The key to such powerful multiple working is the concurrent run-time operating system, which effectively slices up the power of the computer, and allows it to do several things in the same real time. The advent of concurrent run-time versions of such popular P/C operating systems as CP/M will bring significant advances in professional and, eventually, home computer competence in all applications areas but perhaps most fully in WP, which demands the simultaneous running of several programs in order to be fully competent.

4

How to implement WP

Having established the nature and some of the principal benefits of word processing, it is now time to look at how an organisation may go about putting WP technology and techniques into useful practice.

Implementing new technology, especially in an area where little dramatic change has taken place for over a century, apart from the introduction of photocopiers, will never be easy. On the other hand, the advantages of WP, and perhaps its elimination of typing drudgery overall, are immediately obvious to overloaded end users; even poor WP systems have been implemented with splendid effect, simply because *anything* is better than the conventional typewriter.

This section outlines an orderly, sequential approach to the business of implementing new systems, proceeding from examination of the need, through the procurement process to a retroactive appraisal of what actually happened. It ends with some anecdotal warnings (and encouragement). Each organisation will naturally need to develop its own, customized approach to implementation. But, if the general lines of advice in this section are followed, the implementing manager will have the advantage (a) of knowing where he or she is going and (b) that others have successfully been there before.

4.1 SPECIFYING NEEDS

The first logical step in implementing any change, involving computers or otherwise, is to examine the need for change. While any good manager will have developed a sixth sense which transmits the creaks and groans of an ailing system, the extent of the problem and the dimensions of remedial action needed can only be established if some form of objective assessment of current practices and performance is available. This assessment must also be made in terms which not only highlight problems and possibilities for the investigating manager, but also convince those who hold the corporate purse-strings and are probably too well insulated from day-to-day operations to perceive with ease the sounds of strain.

4.1.1 Work measurement and work improvement

The first consideration in looking at conventional systems must be whether a computer-based solution is really justified. It ought to be obvious that computerising an inherently poor system can only result in a bad computer system, probably delivering difficulties a bit quicker. Unfortunately, this is far from universally recognised and – despite 30 years of bitter and better experience with computers – there is *still* a strong tendency to simply transfer current practices and procedures into a computer environment, with predictably less than encouraging results.

Fortunately for potential users of WP, there are a number of intrinsic advantages in the technique, including:

- WP is aimed at delivering an identical end product (text on paper), for which there is an established and continuing need in all organizations
- The English language and the way it is used in commerce and administration are not subject to the same rapid evolution of practice and procedure found in many areas addressed by conventional DP; there is thus a stable basis for technical implementation and development
- end users are attracted by the potential of WP to improve their own working environment, rather than simply as a management productivity tool, and thus rarely have to be cajoled into using it.

Nonetheless, it is also true that any conventional typing operation can be significantly improved by studying current practices and performance and introducing tighter management controls and/or streamlined procedures.

Improvements in throughput of between 30 per cent and 40 per cent have been extracted from typing operations, both through centralising copy typing activities and establishing work flow control, and by putting such improved control procedures to work in already established typing centres. *But,* against this conventional approach, the evidence is that:

- computerization of typing in pools can deliver at least 100 per cent improvements in productivity, chiefly because the machine takes over all repetitive work, and significantly more (200–400 per cent has frequently been recorded) with the right application, such as heavy text drafting
- staff converted to WP do not feel they are having to work significantly harder to achieve the improvement
- no additional human effort needs to be devoted to presentational quality control; a properly designed WP system imposes uniformity in this respect
- at the upper end of the range of productivity increases achieved by work improvement techniques using the same equipment, it is worth noting that such increases have frequently (a) been of short duration and (b) associated directly with highly skilled and motivated individual supervisory staff
- introduction of new technology often provides a vehicle for major reorganization of staff effort which might not be easily acceptable using conventional equipment
- industrial demands for increased payments for using WP have been successfully resisted in several organizations on the demonstrable ground that typing is less demanding than with earlier systems
- computerized WP offers the possibility of automatic collection of statistical management information which it is simply not practicable to amass with conventional machines.

While the evidence is overwhelming that work improvement will never match computerization in the field of word processing, it is nonetheless desirable to carry out at least a theoretical exercise and preferably a small pilot trial to see what might be achieved with conventional machines, in order eventually to use this as the proper baseline for evaluating improvement actually achieved with better hardware.

Work *measurement* is a critical part of any systems improvement exercise; unfortunately many of the skills and disciplines associated with this task were severely eroded or in many organizations disappeared completely during the sustained cost-cutting exercises of the 1970s.

Organization and Methods departments, and Operational Research specialists, once the custodians of performance standards and measures, and designers of streamlined systems, have frequently been phased out of existence (or even phased themselves out, as perhaps their mission indicates they should).

It is, therefore, worth setting down in this document some O&M measurement basics which would have been taken as read in most organizations of 1970.

4.1.2 Performance standards

In order to make continuing measurement meaningful an organization must first find out what current performance looks like, decide if that is adequate, and then set standards which reflect that decision.

Discovering the current status of text production performance is best achieved in the first instance by physical collection of a complete range of typed corporate documentation over a representative period of working time, from a fairly typical section of the organization. Although deciding what 'representative' means in terms of periods of the working year may be difficult, it is usually fairly safe to assume (for the United Kingdom at least) that the best months to measure in are May and October/November, being less upset by annual leave, school and public holidays or staff sickness than the other nine months of the year. A month is a reasonably adequate period to measure, covering a complete internal work cycle in most organizations.

Finding a 'fairly typical' section of any organization is much more of a problem, requiring perhaps somewhat arbitrary definition by someone with long experience of the organization concerned. An alternative solution may be to look for a section or department which carries out a wide spread of all the types of document production practised in the organization. Collecting carbon copies of all paperwork produced during the study period, and having them counted by junior staff, is much easier than asking typists, clerks, technical staff and (especially) managers to conduct themselves counts of pages and words they have written.

Assessing amounts of production must be done in some corporately established standard way. The precise nature of the standard is not absolutely critical, as long as it is universally employed within the organization under study. Counts by line or ethnic word are perfectly acceptable, as long as a standard average line length (say 10 words of seven characters, with six spaces) or word size (say seven characters plus one space) are first defined.

One alternative popular in the 1960s was to identify, using a simple plastic overlay, square inches of page covered by text. A conversion factor (based on line spacing and character size) was then used to establish standard units of typing effort from this very rapidly achieved measurement.

The choice and expression of measurement unit may be left very much to the individual organization, although it will be useful to define this in such a way that performance may be readily compared in similar terms as between one organization and another. Many organizations in the USA and Europe have established various measures and standards, most of which are complex and some of which seek a theoretical precision which is hopelessly unachievable in workaday practice.

A very simplistic rule of thumb for measuring is to assume that the contents of an average sheet of standard office paper will contain:

- roughly 30 lines of text or 300 words (ethnic not computer) if typed at 10 pitch with one clear line left between each typed line (i.e. double-spaced); this is the most frequently found report and letter writing format
- between 50 and 55 lines, containing around 600 words if typed at 12 pitch with no spacing between lines (i.e. single-spaced); this is a typically economy-minded academic/technical report format.

For *throughput/workload* calculation purposes, such pages can be approximately estimated to contain 2,000 actual characters (bytes) in the first instance and 4,000 in the second.

For estimating electronic *storage* needs, some 20 per cent needs to be added to this for spaces between characters and at line ends, plus another amount for control characters used by the system in finding and formatting text. This second overhead varies according to the efficiency with which the system uses and stores control information and actual characters, but will typically be around

20–30 per cent. Typical *storage* needs will thus average around one and a half times the actual number of printable characters held in memory.

This form of measurement naturally focuses on typed *output* in absolute terms as the basis for later comparison of performance.

One school of thought has held that measurement of *input* effort, using established time and motion analyses, was at least equally important. This belief appears to have been frequently accompanied by a philosophy that it was almost cheating to get more out of a system than one put in.

Since the whole point of word processing is to get out of the system far more finished text than one could possibly achieve using conventional input effort, the justification for this approach and philosophy seems slim, especially since the hard work of output counting can be achieved easily by machine after implementation of WP, whereas establishing the exact amount of input effort required, for example, to send a 300-letter mailshot is both a demanding and highly subjective exercise.

Nonetheless, input effort does need to be analysed before standards are set, insofar as the rather subjective question of typing difficulty for various types of documents is concerned. It is, for example, much harder and more time-consuming with a conventional system to type information into a complex form than in free text. Similarly, typing legal documentation, in which no erasure of error is permitted, and where text must go right up to ruled margins in some cases, can be an infuriatingly slow and painstaking process. While WP evens out many of these differences, it is important when setting standards for conventional typing (from which those for WP may later be extrapolated) to allow for these difficulties.

It is advisable to conduct in parallel with line and/or word counts a small series of typing experiments, using a selection of skilled keyboard users, on work of varying difficulty. From the time taken to output a given number of finished words, it may then be deduced what conversion factors should be applied to make, for example, legal typing directly comparable to first-draft audio typing.

On the basis of word/line counts, modified by difficulty factors, standards and/or targets may then be set and promulgated within the organization. The measurement exercise should be repeated at roughly six-monthly intervals, and expanded to include WP systems when they are introduced. In many organizations, such standards have been quickly geared to bonus payments, and form an important factual base for productivity negotiations with staff associations and unions.

4.1.3 Matching operational needs to system facilities

While it ought to be self-evident that systems should be bought on the basis of established operational and business needs rather than hypothetical eventual use, this has historically not always been the case.

Many WP systems have been bought with expensive facilities which the user organization has no expectation of using and which could, in any case, be added later (e.g. list processing, right margination). Others have been acquired without basic facilities essential to the principal application (e.g. inter-document text transfer for large document drafting). So it is vitally important that actual operational needs be very clearly established in the mind of system specifiers, reviewed and agreed *in writing* with their putâtive end users, before the first line of functional specification is written.

The basic questions to be asked must be:

- what functions need to be performed?
- which of these are essential, and which only desirable?
- might any of these functions be more effectively performed with improved conventional systems?
- what computer-based facilities might be offered to perform these functions cost-effectively?
- what are the timescale priorities for implementing the various applications?

4.1.4 Sizing and system requirement

Once a decision is made that a specific group of functions should be converted to word processing techniques, the system specifier should turn to the job of sizing the probable requirement. For project managers, this is second in difficulty only to the ticklish task of estimating software development timetables.

The work measurement exercises outlined earlier in this section should provide a reasonable basis for estimating:

- number of work-stations required
- peaks and troughs of demand for work-section use
- approximate characters input per shift/terminal and output per shift terminal

- characters required to be stored for longer than (say) two weeks.

Further study will be needed to establish:

- how far individual work-station users might be able to share print devices
- communications needs between work-stations.

As a very rough-and-ready check, the following approximations, based on large-scale implementation of WP in many different environments may be made:

- for centralized, shared-resource WP, one work-station will perform the work of two conventional typing stations
- for secretarial typing, two WP terminals sharing a printer will out-perform three conventional typewriters
- one 50 character-per-second printer can comfortably handle the output from four typing stations
- monthly output from 30 conventional typewriters will amount to less than five million characters
- monthly output from 10 WP work-stations will amount to less than 10 million characters (on a properly structured disk system where 70 per cent or more of stored characters are actual alphanumerics and not control characters or packing bytes)
- at least 30 per cent and possibly as much as 90 per cent of all stored text will be transient in nature and may be purged or archived to off-line storage
- in a shared-processor system, used by full-time copy typists, perceptible slowing of system response may generally be looked for around the 10–12 terminal mark, and will get rapidly worse above 16
- where many terminals are sharing the same file handler, response times may be seriously degraded if more than two terminals are in search mode or retrieving/storing large documents at the same time, due to contention for access to disk and data channel transfer speed limitations.

4.1.5 Writing a functional specification

Once the requirement for system facilities, and an approximate sizing of the user need have been set down, it will be necessary to write up this information in a form which can be given with confidence to possible system suppliers. It is *imperative* that this specification constitute an orderly statement, in purely functional terms, of what a system will be required to do. Many costly mistakes have been made because the specifiers, having spent several necessary months familiarizing themselves with matters technical, proceeded prematurely to design a new system in detail instead of specifying its required functions in broad layperson's terms, reinforced by solid numeric detail on the workload.

The functional specification must state very simply and clearly:

- what applications the system will be used for
- approximately how many people are expected to use it, and if work-stations may be shared
- how much information is expected to be input per work-station
- how much information is likely to be output per print device
- how much information requires to be stored (per month) per user, and for how long
- approximate peak loading times (a) by application and (b) by work-station
- what will be regarded as the maximum acceptable response times (a) for inputting (= immediate), (b) retrieving a sizeable document (say, 20 pages), (c) searching for a phrase in a 20-page document and (d) printing out a 20-page document
- where work-stations will be located
- what growth is anticipated in the near future.

This information may then be taken as the basis for elaboration of a Request for Proposal to selected potential suppliers (see section 4.2).

4.2 SEEKING A SOLUTION

Once the need to have a WP system, or network of them, has been established, the detailed functional requirement adequately documented, and a suitable broad allocation of funds prepared in office equipment budget, it is time to go out and seek a supplier to provide a solution. This is likely to be a longish process, unlikely to take less than six months elapsed time as a minimum, unless the prospective user has spent considerable time in informal discussions with a range of likely suppliers in advance of the final decision to do something. Such advance discussion is probably made easiest (and most meaningful for the future) by visiting a couple of trade fairs a year to talk with those suppliers (a) showing anything interestingly new, and (b) used by other organizations in the same line of business as the prospective buyer. This can help shorten considerably the time taken to narrow down the very wide range of system sources to a manageable short-list (see section 4.2.2).

4.2.1 From functional specification to Request for Proposal

It is important for the prospective user going out to tender for any type of computer equipment to obtain replies from suppliers capable of meeting his need which are directly comparable, down to a fairly fine level of detail. In order to achieve this desirable end of being able fairly rapidly to compare like with like in the same context, it will be necessary to prepare for issue a correspondingly detailed and specific document inviting selected suppliers to tender their wares.

The Request for Proposal (RFP) should contain:

- a substantial review of the corporate background to the decision to seek equipment
- the fullest possible text of the functional specification developed in house
- a list of other computer-based equipment used by the prospective buyer, indicating that with which the supplier may be required to interface
- an indication of the extent of required back record conversion and the media on which the records to be converted are stored (e.g. paper, magnetic tape)
- corporate terms and conditions for acquisition of systems and support services
- a draft, user-specified systems acceptance test (or at least notification that such a test *will* be carried out on the basis of criteria defined by the user rather than the supplier).

Given the considerable difficulty, perhaps especially for first-time buyers, of producing a proposal document which all invited suppliers will interpret (and hence respond to) in the same way, it will be useful for the purchaser to invite all suppliers interested in proposing to a joint meeting about (say) three weeks after issue of the tender. This will serve a number of useful purposes, including:

- elimination of suppliers not interested enough to attend or send apologies

- demonstrating whether the functional specification is sufficiently clear, unambiguous and detailed
- allowing suppliers to discuss informally possible pricing barriers
- rapid production of an expanded specification or clarificatory notes for all proposing companies, so that uniformity of response structure is maintained
- generally alerting all interested suppliers to the fact that they are in a competitive situation and should take seriously the preparation of their proposals.

Proposing suppliers should be asked to divide their proposals into three major parts, viz.:

(1) *Technical*

- detailing what equipment is proposed
- showing in detail how the proposal will meet the needs expressed in the functional specification
- adding explanatory or supporting information based on discussion of the proposal with the prospective user
- identifying levels of hardware maintenance and software support to be provided, both on a routine and emergency basis
- specifying duration and levels of training courses and documentation to be provided
- detailing user documentation to be supplied.

(2) *Administrative*

- providing a calendar-related timetable for site preparation, training, installation and acceptance testing
- stating how implementation and support of the system proposed will be organized by the supplier, and the geographical location where the relevant supplier management is based
- identifying what preparatory work for the implementation is the supplier's responsibility and what is expected of the user organization
- detailing how training will be organized.

(3) *Commercial*

- price, itemized for each major hardware component and software modules (unless the software cost is bundled into the overall equipment price)

- payment terms: outright purchase, buyback options, leasing and rental (with notice periods and penalties for cancellation of a rental contract)
- annual support costs for (a) hardware, (b) software
- bulk purchase discount terms and conditions for hardware (and software if applicable)
- cost of cabling unless included in the global equipment price
- fees for training of user staff other than those to be trained free as part of implementation
- charges for new user and systems documentation additional to that supplied at installation
- term of validity of offer
- last three years' financial statements for the supplier company (local company *and* corporate umbrella in the case of large multi-nationals).

Suppliers should be asked to make sure that six copies of their proposal reach the tenders officer of the user organization not later than two months after tender issue date. This gives the suppliers adequate, but not excessive, time and no extension of the response date should be made.

4.2.2 Short-listing suppliers

Suppliers invited to tender should be selected on the basis of three broad criteria: competence of Systems, adequacy of Support and probability of Survival (the 3-S methodology).

Systems competence

Only suppliers with a known track record in the WP systems field should be contacted (at least until a powerful, portable WP package for professional microcomputers with concurrent run-time systems has been on the market for a couple of years and demonstrated its viability).

This list should be further narrowed down by

- determining those suppliers with known high competence in the specific WP applications (e.g. list processing) which the user needs most
- talking to existing users of supplier products to eliminate the less competent/reliable
- (ideally) short-term trial of two or three small systems from selected suppliers.

Support adequacy
The only reliable guide here is to talk with existing customers of short-listed suppliers and gain a comprehensive view of their likely performance. This examination should relate to geographical areas remote from as well as close to the prospective user organization, so that depth and spread of coverage can be properly appreciated.

The purchaser should ascertain where the bulk of the supplier's hardware and software development staff are located, and make an independent judgment as to whether this proximity is commercially adequate or not (the 'comfort factor') for the future.

Survival quotient
It will be disappointing (to say the least) if the first generation of WP system bought from a supplier should turn out to be the last. The prospective buyer should examine the survival prospects of possible suppliers by:

- looking at their past five years' business performance and growth rate in the world at large (not just home territory)
- determining their investment in and facilities for forward systems development, including plans for upgrading hardware and existing software
- looking at the range, and especially internal upward compatibility, of hardware and software products offered by the vendor
- examining a given supplier's dependence on sub-contractors, and arrangements for second sourcing of equipment in the event of failure of one or more sub-contractors.
- reviewing in detail the quality of the promotional, user and technical documentation offered by suppliers; failing suppliers don't write good books.

Given the sometimes excessively dynamic nature of the information systems market, allied to the fact that not even the biggest supplier can any longer wholly guarantee his survival in the same form, it is likely that a prospective purchaser may feel moved to examine the offerings of one or more less than firmly established offering companies. If this is so, three other fail-safe criteria will apply:

- are the staff, products and development concepts of this company sufficiently attractive to be bought in by a more financially stable organization in the event of business problems? (in which case, don't worry too much)

- if they should collapse, can hardware spares and software development tools be obtained elsewhere?
- who are the principal investors other than the company management?

4.2.3 Contractual terms and conditions

Most suppliers will seek to impose their own contractual terms and conditions on customers, while those organizations which have developed their own rules for systems acquisition will respond by endeavouring to impose their own. In practice, the resulting contract is usually a compromise between the two.

Any organization coming new to the acquisition of computerized office equipment will be well advised to look at some of the tougher contractual provisions whose adoption large user organizations usually succeed in imposing on those wishing to do serious business with them. A particularly widely emulated (and recommendable) set of terms and conditions is that used by Her Majesty's Stationery Office for controlling Governmental offices systems purchasing.

While normal consumer precautions will give a resonable guarantee in buying, leasing, or renting WP systems, it is particularly important to watch a number of specific points in contract drafting, including:

- liability for physical damages in the event of major system malfunction (fire, etc.)
- exact point of handover of insurance liability for systems being installed; does the supplier's insurance cover a machine all the way to the user's office floor, or only as far as the works exit, or the user's trade entrance, etc.?
- indemnification of the user by the supplier against any proceedings relating to patent or copyright infringements by the supplier or his agents
- who is responsible for any unforeseen delay in installation, what are the penalties and what constitutes *force majeure*?
- does the buyer have the right to offer the equipment and/or software for re-sale, and under what constraints (e.g. could it be sold to COMECON countries).
- for how long does the supplier guarantee to provide hardware spares and support software releases?
- does the user have to adopt new releases of software or can he

insist that the supplier support earlier releases if these were more reliable or relevant?
- what is the supplier's guaranteed response time in the event of system failure, and what will the cost supplement be if this response is out of normal working hours (and how are these defined)?
- nomination of an arbitrator who may be expected to know enough about the technicalities of WP systems to deliver an informed verdict in the event of a dispute rooted in technical problems
- under what circumstances has the supplier the right to refuse to cease supporting the system(s) (e.g. unsupervised removal to another site, attachment of non-approved peripherals, etc.)?
- confidentiality: protection of user organization information against possible intrusion by outside agents with the connivance of supplier staff; conversely, protection of the supplier against unauthorized disclosure of development or performance information to competitors
- protection of the user and supplier against 'poaching' of skilled staff.

4.3 EVALUATION AND PURCHASE

Evaluation of supplier responses to an invitation to tender for the supply of WP systems is a heavy task, which will be impossibly complex unless a very tightly structured proposal is demanded (see section 4.2). Even then, it is inevitable that suppliers will have chosen to interpret many matters of detail in ways best suited to the products they have on offer.

To obtain some kind of independent judgment on the relative value of the offerings, while keeping a close eye on the subjective needs of the prospective purchaser, it is necessary to adopt an evaluation methodology. This methodology should combine objectively identifiable elements of system and supplier competence with differential weightings assigned to those elements subjectively, in the light of their known relative values to the buyer organization.

This section therefore outlines how to construct tables of selection criteria and sub-criteria, weight each sub-criterion, and arrive at a demonstrably logical basis for final decision-making, which takes into account very directly the extent to which the respective systems proposed will meet the needs they are intended to address. In the long run, the decision may still come down to intuitive judgment between two (or maybe three) contenders whom it is still difficult to separate, reinforced, naturally, by their final reaction to efforts to squeeze out the best commercial deal – a topic also addressed in this section.

4.3.1 Detailed schedule of evaluation criteria

The same three broad sets of evaluation criteria are proposed as were used to whittle down the list of potential suppliers to those who were actually asked to bid: system competence, support, and supplier survival. To these a fourth should now be added: selling price. For the evaluation exercise, the first two of the original three criteria must be broken down into more detailed sub-criteria, perhaps along the following lines:

System competence

- extent of basic editing repertoire
- closeness of match between advanced editing packages and identified user needs
- adaptability of applications by the user
- simplicity of user interface
- range and size of storage options
- efficiency of retrieval mechanisms
- range of print device options
- probable perceived speed of system response
- management and housekeeping facilities
- confidentiality and security mechanisms
- background printing and communications
- reliability, in terms of anticipated mean time between failure (MTBF) based on supplier statistics
- incremental costs of system expansion
- field-upgradeability of system/sub-systems
- 'graceful degradation' in the event of partial systems failure
- compatibility with other system types (a) from the chosen supplier, and (b) from other suppliers.

Supplier support

- promised maximum response time
- location of personnel – hardware
  - software
  - development

- cost of new software releases
- cost of any special software development
- adequacy of spares holdings
- forward development plans
- readiness to assist with interfacing to other supplier's systems.

The examination of *supplier survival* at the time of short-listing should take care of most of the investigation needed here, but these factors should be re-introduced and weighted.

To the question of price should be added possible extra costs attributable to:

- provision of backup facilities (obviously potentially greater in the case of highly centralized configurations, for example)
- additional site preparation costs required for large central/ shared units (e.g. air conditioning, anti-static carpeting)
- acoustical hoods for printers
- abnormally high consumable costs (e.g. special printer ribbons, chemically treated paper required)
- excessively high electrical power consumption.

4.3.2 Weighted ranking techniques

Having established the key criteria for the evaluation exercise, the project manager(s) and users in the buyer organization should then agree individual weightings for these and other organization-specific criteria. To make the exercise mathematically straightforward, it is suggested that the total weights add up to a large round figure such as 100, with (say) 50 per cent of the weight assigned to system competence, 20 per cent to support 20 per cent to supplier survivability and 10 per cent to cost. (Provided that price quotations are all within the same general area, after the checks and balances outlined earlier in this section are made, this factor can be virtually eliminated. Price should be regarded as much less important than the risk of total project failure.) Each bulk percentage is then further divided up among the sub-criteria, which are assigned sub-percentages by the user organization's evaluation panel. Supplier proposals are then given marks (percentages of the percentages i.e.) and their totals added up.

If there is no clear victor (and there are likely to be two or three close contenders), the evaluation panel may then shift the broad criterion weightings and/or the sub-criterion weights to determine if the marks of any of the close contenders are badly affected by a shift in areas which the panel considers of arguably greater importance (e.g. supplier survival). Experience indicates that this secondary-phase weight-shifting exercise is likely to produce a final candidate, or at most two.

4.3.3 Negotiating the best deal

Small users

Small users, i.e. those unlikely to purchase more than (say) £100,000 worth of equipment in a budget year, can get the best deal out of a given supplier in one of a number of ways, including:

- determining what their likely long-term maximum commitment to purchases will be, and negotiating a discount rate based on that total, with individual purchases 'called off' at intervals against that total; armed with a letter of intent confirming the higher figure, many organizations will offer conditional bulk discount deals
- teaming up with other interested purchasers in a group-buying arrangement amounting to a closed dealership, and then approaching the supplier for good bulk discount terms; this has already been done effectively in the UK where, for example, HMSO buys at substantial discounts on behalf of national and local administration clients and the universities have four major regional agencies for systems procurement
- offering the supplier free workshop space for system repairs and spares holdings to serve nearby organizations other than the prime user; this may be particularly attractive to a supplier wishing to have a resident engineer in a sparsely covered location, but unable so far to justify the cost of premises. For the host organization, this has the additional advantage of giving them effectively a resident engineer.

Large users

Large users are in a strong position to bargain. Even IBM, who long refused to give any discount, will now negotiate bulk-purchase deals.

A really large buyer can arrange to become effectively an OEM (original equipment manufacturer) factoring house, enjoying discounts of 40 per cent and often considerably more from the normal one-off price. Multi-nationals who decide to standardize on a short-list of approved suppliers can get even better deals, particularly if they are prepared to allow the supplier to advertise major installations and/or use them as reference sites for prospective buyers to visit.

Most large organizations can also insist on having a dedicated site support engineer or team for each major site, once they get near or beyond approximately 50–60 work-stations in that site. Many suppliers reckon around this number of work-stations to be the breakeven point where support revenue cancels out the direct cost of a permanent engineer. Since the support of additional terminals will add only marginal cost, supporting a resident engineer can be seen as seed money for business growth in the general area of the site where he resides, and a good sales-oriented engineer will in any case help to generate more business in the host organization. The user organization then benefits by getting a bulk deal for site support rather than paying the standard rate for each system supported.

Large organizations also have a strong case for substantial reduction in the price of new software releases or packaged products.

4.4 SITE PREPARATION

Planning and preparation for installation of new WP systems should begin as soon as possible after the decision on general configuration (centralized or distributed) is taken. Even if stand-alone units with no shared central resources are planned, a certain amount of preparation of the site where they are to be installed will be needed. Where bigger units of central hardware are concerned, or if any of them need air conditioning, the scheduling of preparatory work at the chosen site assumes a critical nature. It is not unknown for large quantities of equipment to have to wait in a storeroom at a user site while electrical and construction work are completed so that they can be used. Such a slippage in overall project timescales can be highly deleterious to (a) budgetary appropriations, (b) end user morale and (c) corporate confidence in the competence of the project manager.

This section offers advice on how to avoid unforeseen delays attributable to site preparation, and details necessary safety precautions for any major installation.

Once a final short-list of potential suppliers is drawn up, it will be advisable to invite each tendering supplier to visit the site(s) involved and detail in his proposal any special problems or requirements, and the likely cost of meeting them. On the safety front, all suppliers should be asked to state in their proposals what safety standards are met by their equipment, and final contractual documents (both for system acquisition and support) must contain an undertaking by the supplier that all equipment supplied, replacement parts and any electrical work carried out by him or his agents will meet full safety standards.

4.4.1 Physical requirements

Given the continually reducing weight and size of computer equipment and the increasingly varied roles which computerized telecommunication systems are being assigned, it seems entirely possible that, by 1990, site preparation will consist of little more than clearing a foot-square space on the user's desk, (always supposing, of course, that users still have desks rather than simply using perhaps a highly portable, multi-function terminal placed on a swing-in plane surface attached to the armrest of a comfortable chair).

For the time being (i.e. roughly 1985–88) it is likely that the following check-list will take care of most of the important elements of any major WP installation:

Space

- terminals (CRT-based): desktop area approximately two feet (60 cm) wide by three feet (90 cm) deep, to allow for individual choice in positioning separable keyboards. Desk tops should be four centimetres lower than standard (68 cm rather than 72) to drop the keyboard to a comfortable height, or a conventional typing return of this height should be fitted. The desktop will need to be six inches (15 cm) deeper than the normal two feet six inches (75 cm). Desks do not need to be wider than four feet (120 cm) compared with the more normal 5 ft 6 inches (165 cms) 5 ft 10 inches (175 cm) or 6 ft (180 cm), unless a processor and/or disk drive box is to be mounted underneath the working surface.
- large microcomputers and large (80MB +) disk drives need a floor area three feet square with an additional 20 inches (50 cm) at front and back to allow for service access.

Power supply

- although many systems now use a single plug for all work-station elements, including a printer, each work-station should have at least two and preferably three 13-amp three-pin power sockets close at hand, or even built into the furniture

– ideally, the power supply will be provided by a separate take-off from the central mains. WP equipment should not be placed on the same circuit (or at least not close on the same local loop) as photocopiers, lift motors or other major items of electrical equipment producing heavy surge demands for current. If access is feasible to computer room power supplies, this will be ideal
– a clean earth should be provided for all WP equipment
– while all WP equipment is normally protected against power fluctuations of around plus or minus 10 per cent, the circuit used should be protected against massive spikes (current surges) or 'hard' (sudden) cuts, preferably by supplying power to equipment from a battery system which is normally kept continuously topped up from the mains. This will prevent damage to electronic components and the internal power supply in the event of a major fluctuation
– if there is a strong likelihood that equipment will be moved at frequent intervals, consideration should be given to providing a false floor for power and communications connections. If a new building is involved, it can actually be cheaper to install false flooring than lay conventional tiles and carpets
– a central circuit breaker should be provided for all large central processors or sub-systems.

Communications

– computer work-stations are increasingly linked by twisted-pair (i.e. like telephone wire) cables or (and this may become the norm) fibre-optic cables. Either of these will have a diameter of about one fifth of an inch (half a centimetre), which needs to be allowed for in cable trunking. If coaxial cable is used, this will have a diameter of around 0.9 inch (2.25 cms)
– communications links will be multi-channel and only one need be allowed for per work-station
– twisted-pair or coaxial cable should be separated in trunking from any power cables by at least three inches, to prevent possible data corruption by magnetic induction effects. Fibre-optic transmission cable is impervious to these.

Air conditioning

Most modern computer equipment can survive a fairly wide range of temperature variations and cope with reasonable levels of foreign matter in the air. Large disk units may still need some filtering (ideally to eliminate any foreign object larger than 0.05 microns) and cooling.

Full air conditioning to computer-room standards is usually expensive, and its effects on other building systems unpredictable. It needs a separate pre-installation study, and consideration of the possibility of using much cheaper window-mounted or even free-standing cooler units. It is also worth noting that, while equipment may be able to stand a degree or two of overheating, the people who work round large heat sources may not (and should not have to).

Large, free-standing units will need consideration in designing/directing overall cooling airflows. The effects of these units and, to a certain extent, individual work-stations on the temperature and humidity (or lack of it) in an open-plan working environment are difficult to estimate in advance. It may be necessary to consult an architect specializing in open-plan air conditioning.

4.4.2 Safety precautions

Floor loading

Computer equipment has decreased very substantially in physical weight, and continues to do so. Large, side-loading disk drive units still, however, tend to have substantial counterweights built in, and a twin-drive unit can weigh as much as 500 lbs.

Load-spreading feet for disk-drive cabinets can lower the point load to well within safe point-loading limits, but this needs always to be double-checked.

Fire precautions

Hand-held *dry* chemical extinguishers are recommended for work-stations and stand-alone systems. For larger, central configurations, halogen-gas systems connected to smoke and heat detectors may be required; the supplier should be asked to recommend an adequate level of extinguisher.

All security copies of disks and at least one copy of all systems documentation should be kept in a fire-resistant cabinet which will withstand at least 30 minutes intense heat without melting or charring its contents.

Any large central computer rooms should have glass bolts to ensure easy egress for occupants; breaking these bolts should trigger building fire alarms.

Flood

Present-day computer equipment is far more resistant to the effects of water than its predecessors, but electrical components and conventional cabling are still vulnerable. Equipment and cabling should be located as far as possible away from water sources, and (ideally) water escape ducts/vents should be interposed between the nearest source and the equipment or cables. (N.B. fibre-optic cables are unaffected by water.)

Power supplies

All equipment must be properly earthed, and (with connectors and plugs) be certified to British safety standards. If British certification is not immediately available, equivalent U.S. or West German (the most stringent currently known) safety clearance *must* be available. In case of any doubt, it is worth consulting the Government-sponsored Central Computer and Telecommunications Agency (CCTA) at Riverside Walk in central London, which has a Division specializing in computer equipment safety.

Electro-mechanical and laser equipment

Many electro-mechanical printers have quite violent print-head return mechanisms and fast-moving paper feeds, while laser printers may have internal shielding which should only be removed by a qualified technician.

All equipment with moving parts or using lasers should have appropriate, easily seen warning labels affixed to or or close by.

4.5 INSTALLATION AND ACCEPTANCE

System installation is the high point of any information technology implementation project, needing continuous attendance and attention by the project manager for the first few critical days. It is also the commercial crunch-point at which supplier promises must be turned into deliverables, rigorously checked and approved (or sent back) by the user organization's delegated representative. Planning is again essential.

Ideally, user and supplier should nominate specific individuals to manage the implementation from both sides of the emptor/vendor fence. These two should meet as soon as possible after the decision is taken to entrust supply to a specific supplier (or prime contractor, in the event of a very large, multi-sourced project). Their first task is to elaborate a plan detailing all work to be done up to and including the date of installation.

The user organization's manager must also draw up, and can usefully pass to the supplier's representative, a detailed system acceptance test based on the functional specification contained in the Request for Proposal. By the installation date, this specification (with modifications) should have been firmly integrated into the supplier's contractual undertaking to deliver a competent system to meet the user's need.

4.5.1 Installation

The Installation Plan will vary according to user organization, and may quite possibly be based on the supplier's standard installation plan (most serious suppliers have an installation guide-book). It should, however, contain at least the following elements:

- date and instructions for early, detailed site survey(s) and report from supplier (if this has not been done at the proposal stage)
- final determination of work-station and central equipment locations (where applicable)
- (proceeding from the two above elements) specific cable lengths required
- office furniture requirement/procurement details
- briefing for electrical contractors, including dates for work to be finished
- briefing for builders, including finish dates
- instructions for building security and maintenance staff and porters for use on installation day(s)
- training schedule for user staff (see section (4.6)
- check that equipment to be installed has comfortable clearance through doors and passages to installation site, and does not exceed permitted lift loadings (where applicable)
- check that loading bays and lifts will be available on installa-

tion date(s), especially if a weekend installation is planned (when canteen or other refreshment facilities should also be available)
- double-check continuity of system and accident insurance coverage
- sequenced timetable for equipment delivery and engineer attendance
- (ideally) alternative draft timetable for use in the event of unforeseen hitches.

4.5.2 Acceptance test

Most suppliers will wish to conduct a system acceptance test as soon as possible after equipment delivery and connection, for the very cogent reason that payment for the goods is almost invariably made contractually contingent on such tests.

While major items of equipment should have been 'burned in' during 'soak testing' at the supplier's premises for a week or ten days prior to delivery, moving equipment can cause physical hardware problems which must be exorcised before system testing can begin. Suppliers will usually conduct a rigorous test of hardware and *basic* software within half a day or so. But all that test proves is that (a) the equipment is now assembled in reasonably good shape (b) the operating system is in reasonable control of the sub-systems it is supposed to control.

Complete performance of all the functions required in the user specification must now be fully exhibited. Since this, to be wholly meaningful, will require participation of the end user population, and almost certainly take up several days, it is prudent to plan for a two-stage acceptance test:

Stage I by the supplier, demonstrating basic hardware and software competence
Stage II by user staff, giving the system a thorough workout and reporting in detail on all difficulties or failures. This could well last a week.

Most suppliers will find it not unreasonable to take a conditional acceptance at the satisfactory conclusion of Stage I, allowing their accounting department to get on with invoicing. The user can then withhold payment of invoices at least until he is happy with the Stage II performance.

The user acceptance test must be written down, and should be expanded or elaborated in real time if areas of doubt or lack of clarity are discovered during preliminary testing.

4.6 TRAINING

Training for the introduction of advanced WP in an organization which has little or no experience of computerized office systems implies an education much broader than that of simply the end user typists.

It has commonly been found that keyboard specialists very rapidly acquire the new skills and habits required, and are glad to do so. The loudest complaints about any new system will tend to come from *indirect* users, i.e. authors, more often than not because they feel they do not understand how it works and cannot therefore take full and immediate advantage of the benefits it offers.

Where a large, centrally controlled, implementation is envisaged, it is also likely that non-technical staff required to manage the new production machinery will need very careful education, closely geared to individual learning curves. Appropriate levels of direct user training and background familiarization for indirect users are therefore essential to the successful launch of a new system and rapid enhancement of its productivity.

Suppliers will usually undertake, as part of the all-up contract price, to train a given number of direct users, but other forms of education are most often left to the end user to devise and organize. This section sets out some of the important considerations for all types of training and education.

4.6.1 Trials and pilot systems

Perhaps the best way for any user organization to learn rapidly and effectively about the way new systems will work and affect work processes is to take the pragmatic 'suck-it-and-see' approach, with a trial or pilot system.

The essential distinction between trials and pilots lies largely in the semantics and philosophy of risk analysis:

- a trial system can be thrown out with little financial loss (several suppliers offer free or at-cost short-term trials)

– a pilot is intended to act as the pattern (albeit one which can be modified) for widespread later implementation of the same type of solution.

In practice, there is often very little difference in timescale, cost or follow-up between an extended trial and a short-term pilot. The quality of experience gained with either type of preliminary implementation will probably not vary much either. It is, however, debatable how many trial systems can be thrown out before the putative user population becomes disenchanted with the prospect of computer-based word processing.

There is no doubt at all, however, that either a trial or pilot exercise constitutes excellent preparation of user project managers for much greater things and gives them a deep insight into the quality and practices of their supplier.

If bad mistakes are to be made (and some will almost inevitably be when treading new ground), it is clearly preferable from every viewpoint that they be confined to microcosmic proportions rather than seriously disturbing the whole corporate macrocosm.

From the end user viewpoint, provided they are kept clearly informed and reminded that what they have now must be critically examined before it becomes the corporate norm, hands-on experience of *any* WP equipment is invaluable. As long as any subsequent solution is demonstrably better than what they have tried, such experience will lead to much quicker acceptance and familiarity with the new solution.

4.6.2 End user familiarization and training

The most critical aspect of training end users is not to give them too much or too little information at one time. For complete WP beginners, too much information can be bewildering and cause great apprehension (and misapprehension too!). On the other hand, typists who already have exposure to electronic editing typewriters or have used earlier generation WP machines usually cannot wait to get their hands on a new machine, and will rapidly teach themselves if given adequate information. They can get very irritated with trainers who are slow to realize this and adapt their methods to meet it.

Training programmes should ideally combine several levels of activity for the learner:

- generalized reading about the system before its delivery
- hands-on familiarization either at the supplier's premises or with another user organization
- one day's directly supervised keyboard training, followed by two days' supervised education in the use of all non-supervisory functions
- two or three weeks of self-teaching, supported by a training program on disk and/or an audio tape
- final test and certification (an important morale boosting detail) after about one month.

Detailed user documentation should not be made available to a typist until the first three days of supervised training are successfully completed. Before these three days, the typist should be given a two or three-page summary of basic keyboard functions as an outline guide to use. Documentation for end users should be a judicious mixture of in-house procedural guidance and more technical materials supplied by the user.

Very few suppliers provide really user-friendly documentation, and it will probably be advisable for a deep introductory chapter to be written in-house, preferably by a senior typist with some experience of the new system or at least of word processing techniques in general.

Supervisory staff will need deeper training from the supplier. The extent and nature of this will depend very directly on the type of system chosen, and the scope and sophistication of its housekeeping and management facilities.

An important point in early training of end user and supervisory staff will concern reporting of system faults and failures. For clarity and effectiveness of user-supplier communication, this should be channelled through a single user representative to a single, clearly identified supplier executive. End users should be taught to record failures in detail, especially early on after implementation when the system and its users are settling down. This will assist the supplier very considerably in taking remedial and preventative action; it will probably also prevent the reporting of imaginary faults.

On the more positive side, end user staff should equally be motivated to report useful hints and tips on easier (and inevitably more effective) ways to use system facilities. Within a month of the arrival of any new system, end user staff will usually have found at least a dozen better ways of using it for some particular purpose than the supplier could have imagined. The user organization should cash in on this inevitable inventiveness.

4.6.3 Indirect user education

Text originators need to feel associated from a very early stage with the introduction of new WP systems although, unlike the direct users, they should probably not be intensively consulted about the detailed functional specification. Short presentations and seminars, with substantial time allowed for question-and-answer sessions, should be given at intervals once a decision has been made to have any new system. Once a supplier and specific system type are chosen, these sessions can be more directly related to the equipment and software actually to be introduced, possibly with the participation of supplier specialists.

General office systems educational films are a considerable help in allaying fears and suspicions, and will increase in value as the organization proceeds towards a greater degree of integrated automation in the office. Inviting direct and indirect users to such sessions together can also help to promote a more understanding working relationship in the event of possible early difficulties with a new system. Many suppliers offer semi-promotional training films and videotapes linked to their own products, and a substantial number of less product-linked productions have been made since the early 1970s. Among the best of these, driving home important points with memorable faces, voices, and some excellent situation comedy, are those from Video Arts, which feature John Cleese and other well known TV performers.

Project managers should also use where feasible the educational talents of their own staff. In the late 1970s, for example, ICI made one of the best general-purpose educational films yet seen on the benefits of organized WP, starring its own staff on their own machines and directed by an ICI executive.

Acquisition of at least a couple of videotape recorder/players and one CCTV camera to use with them is highly advisable, as also the use from time to time of 16 mm film projectors.

Apart from the conventional indirect use of new typing facilities by authors i.e. by sending their manuscript or audio dictation to a secretary or pool supervisor, there is emerging of new class of 'semi-direct' user among text originators.

Many organizations have found that, once WP is installed, authors with urgent needs to move text rapidly will seek to sit down at a terminal and grapple quickly and directly with the correction process. While it may well be a long time (if ever) before most authors will do bulk inputting of text, it seems very probable that, as simpler user interfaces continue to evolve and work-station functionality becomes increasingly catholic, the bulk of indirect users will quite soon wish to do simple revise-editing of text entered for them by an amanuensis. A cut-down, simplified training schedule oriented towards their needs should be developed, ideally with the assistance of an author-oriented program on disk. It needs to do little more than teach them the rudiments of character and line correction, insertion and deletion, plus how to retrieve a document from store and put it back afterwards.

4.7 SYSTEMS INTEGRATION

While many organizations will launch into WP and other forms of office system with one or two scattered terminal clusters or stand-alone machines, in a relatively short time most of them will be looking to integrate these into a more comprehensive corporate information handling system. It is a regrettable fact of mid-1980s life that this is likely to present considerable difficulties unless all the systems chosen are from the same supplier, or from a very limited list of suppliers who have convincingly demonstrated inter-working between their products.

Even where standards for inter-*communication* exist – several do and more detailed ones are emerging – suppliers very often interpret these in different ways which result in inability to inter-*work* effectively with other machines. Files may be transferable from one system type to another, for example, but cannot be processed on the receiving machine without considerable software development. This is even true in some cases with systems from the same manufacturer, produced by different divisions and design teams. Fortunately for the end user of 1990, things are beginning to improve. Manufacturers are increasingly recognizing that no single supplier can be all things to all men. They are also aware that the overall market (and consequently their particular slice of it) is liable to be substantially increased by standardisation to a level which allows discerning users to buy the most appropriate systems and sub-systems without regard to supplier, and then link them together. The very rapid escalation in the facsimile market which followed telecommunications standardization for these devices has served as a powerful and encouraging example of this.

Better-defined standards are beginning to emerge, with less loopholes for accidental or deliberate misinterpretation. Significantly, the most directly relevant of these for WP (Normalized Document Format – see below) is the result of an initiative by manufacturers not users or established international standards bodies. Perhaps even more promisingly for the eventual integrated electronic office, a new standard is being adopted *de facto* (and *ab initio*) by the bulk of manufacturers interested in supplying communicating graphics systems.

Standards which seem likely to have a large part to play in bringing about the integrated office of 1990 include:

- Teletex: developed primarily by European telecommunications authorities as a basis for enhanced telex machines with full WP capability, this emerging standard (a) defines a pan-European characters set of over 300 characters, which goes on to specify standard graphic elements, and (b) defines fairly tightly format controls for presenting a page of text. It represents the first standard for text communication likely to be widely applied since Telex itself, which can only handle upper-case characters, numbers and a very small range of figures (and is not 100 per cent universally adopted!)
- NDF: Normalized Document Format. This definition of the way document formats should be communicated in standard from derives from a British Telecom exercise started in 1980, to design a universal office systems communications interface called ALBERT. As part of this exercise, the British consultancy Logica developed the Albert Standard Document Format. This was later developed further by Logica and International Computers Ltd (ICL), and submitted to the European Computer Manufacturers Association (ECMA) to be further developed and presented to the international standards bodies as at least a European standard. It goes beyond the teletex specification, chiefly in addressing whole documents rather than single pages but also in still more detailed definition of format controls
- IBM: the predominance of the world's largest computer supplier has historically meant that its communications protocols and formatting standards have achieved *de facto*

adoption by a large number of other suppliers, simply because most large organizations have a number of big IBM machines somewhere fairly important in the corporate apparatus. This quasi-hegemony has not yet been seen in the office systems field because IBM have not achieved anything like the pre-eminence in word processing that they enjoy in DP; WANG has dominated the market and continues at the time of writing to do so. It is nevertheless true that most WP systems given the facility to converse with any machine other than their own supplier's kind have been given IBM 2780 or 3270 capability before anything else.

IBM have developed their own document format, once known as DCF (document content format) and more lately ODA (office document architecture) since DCF has at least three other meanings within IBM and one much more generally outside (discounted cash flow). This definition is not entirely alien to the NDF proposals, and IBM are understood to have attended ECMA meetings progressing NDF as observers during 1983. Hopefully, the two will be merged to give the first truly comprehensive standard for expressing the way documents are put together and enabling them to be communicated between and processed by a whole host of different system types

- ISO/DIN: the International Standards Organization (ISO) and the German Standards Institution (DIN) have painstakingly drafted and put forward for international adoption a character-fount standard ISO/DIN 6937. This embraces the whole range of characters covered by Teletex, and goes further, out to 512 characters and symbols. It also provides for the development of standard sub-sets for difficult character and symbol ranges, such as advanced mathematical conventions
- X25: likely to be adopted universally in Europe, and already defined as a corporate communications baseline by many large commercial organizations and European bodies, X25 defines in detail seven layers of control for information being transmitted on large networks, ranging from simple hardware connection through transport mechanisms to basic format controls.

4.8 POST-IMPLEMENTATION AUDIT

Once a system is installed and the first few (usually hectic) days of live working and instant learning are over, it will be highly desirable for the project manager to sit down and begin planning his/her first audit of the new system's performance. Periodic audits of this kind should be carried out as a kind of series of snapshots in a family album, to show how well the new child is growing and developing.

The first audit should be carried out jointly by the implementation project manager and the person(s) responsible for day-to-day management of the new system(s), in consultation with the supplier's implementation executive. Subsequent audits should probably be carried out by an auditing functionary less directly involved with either project planning or routine management of the system(s).

4.8.1 Aims of the audit

The information derived from the audit will be crucial to forward development of the overall corporate information processing system, since it should:

- determine levels of improvement in text production (quantitatively *and* qualitatively)
- examine, for future reference, how close the improvement achieved came to that which was planned
- identify areas of system performance needing improvement
- produce a record of supplier performance in both implementation and support
- highlight facilities or equipment which are inadequate as installed, or which it would be useful to add to the system
- enable management to set new standards for performance which can be used as the basis for estimating future systems requirements
- deliver very germane assistance in tackling the problem of sizing future systems
- generally furnish the factual basis for retroactive justification of the first installation (see section 5), leading to confidence in budgeting for the next.

4.8.2 Areas to be studied

The audit should look in detail wherever possible statistics generated by (or at least available within) the management facilities of the system(s), at the following areas:

- individual work-station performance, differentiating between

amounts of work input and output, in standard corporate measurement units
- total system output, in direct comparison with the situation before installation
- peaks and troughs of workload (a) by work-station, and (b) overall
- percentage availability of the whole system(s) = time working as a percentage of time when the system was required to be working
- MTBF (mean time between failure) of sub-systems and central resources
- MTTR (mean time to repair) = average time support personnel take to fix a problem, measured from the time the fault is reported and (ideally) from the repairman's arrival on site
- evidence of overlong response times, excessive re-tries for disk access
- any indication of data loss or corruption
- time occupied in housekeeping activities
- consumables throughput rate (ribbons, toner, print wheels, paper, etc.)
- any evidence of increased requests for re-editing
- (where applicable) percentages of documents communicated
- size and nature of information stored archivally
- frequency of use of standard forms/text modules
- print quality (including imprint blackness for photocopying or offset litho masters)
- accident and incident logs.

4.9 DOs AND DONTs

Finally, to round off this section for new users on how to implement WP, a few hints, tips and awful warnings drawn from the installation of a large number of WP systems in a great variety of working environments.

4.9.1 DO

- involve end users as early as possible in system specification and design. They are the experts, and even the best system in the world will not do as well as it might if its users don't feel committed to its use
- spend a lot of time talking to WP system users and interest

groups with a communal store of experience both before your first implementation and on a continuing basis afterwards. The British Computer Society has a special WP specialist group, and the International Word Processing Association's UK chapter welcomes newcomers; many suppliers also have national and regional user groups where users can both pool experience and exert pressure on the supplier to make specific developments and generally improve his performance
- make sure everything your supplier promises gets written down and incorporated into your purchase contract
- plan ahead in detail, and make sure all corporate decision-makers know in good time precisely what you are planning; avoid surprises . . .
- educate everybody involved with the introduction of new systems in what to expect, at *their* level of expectation
- organize the logging of all incidents and events with a newly installed system
- watch for changes in the way people work after the introduction of new WP systems
- keep a central log of job directories for all off-line archival recording media
- make sure the author agrees before deleting a long-stored document.

4.9.2 DON'T

- overload trainees with teaching or text. One very bright, mature lady once nearly had a nervous breakdown, lost 10 nights of sleep and lagged way behind her much younger co-trainees because somebody gave her a technical supervisor's manual long before she should have had it. She learned this weighty document off by heart, recited chunks of its text in panic when she found even simple typing defeated her. Only the trainer's final realization of what was wrong, and removal of the offending text eventually allowed her to calm down. She then took to WP keyboarding in five minutes (literally), and eventually became an excellent large-system supervisor.
- let end users in centralized systems invent job names at random, unless the central file control and retrieval system are pretty powerful. An early user of shared-logic systems ran into a lot of trouble because the main initial application was

typing purchase orders, and all eleven typists on the first system decided that PO + sequential number was the logical name for such documents. The system supervisor had considerable difficulty sorting out something like 150 X 11 sets of documents called PO at the end of week 1

- leave passwords written down where any intruder can find them; conversely, do encourage the supervisor to write them down *somewhere,* just in case she falls sick or under the legendary Mack Truck
- assume there is any logical or direct relationship between minutes of recorded audio direction and the number of words in an audio record. People speak at different rates, cough, interrupt to make asides and often correct a single paragraph four or five times
- always tell typing staff the precise basis on which their work is being measured. The O&M manager of a large company in the travel business once claimed to have invented the most accurate system of job measurement ever devised, and to be persuading a phenomenal average of over 550 lines a day out of temporary typists. It turned out that his averages were based on spot checks on Thursday afternoons, the typists discovered this and contrived to deliver 300 lines after lunch each Thursday and earn their bonus; the rest of the week was anybody's guess
- assume that WP is only good for specific applications. Once it's installed, use it for everything reasonable – even sticky labels
- presume that WP must necessarily out-perform conventional systems in every environment. One US Department of Defense typing centre introduced new work flow control management procedures, threw out its (admittedly basic) word processors and improved performance by 20 per cent. A large railway company lost 15 per cent productivity with a highly competent WP system as against electric machines because the users had not been convinced that automation was a good idea
- take it for granted that apparent simplicity of instruction necessarily guarantees understanding. The supervisor of a new WP system in a large manufacturing concern found great difficulty in her first attempt to take security copies of her system disks. The menu display said: 'Now type: COPY AAAAAA Drive 1 to BBBBBB Drive 2'. As neither of her disks were

called AAAAAA or BBBBBB, she tried in vain until it was pointed out to her that she should substitute the names of *her* disks for the AAAAAA or BBBBBB

– allow end users to determine whether a system has crashed or not. The first day's operational use of one large system came to an abrupt halt after 10 minutes when all eight screens went dead. After another 10 minutes of soothing talk, the supplier's support manager succeeded in establishing over the phone that the CPU and disks appeared to be working well. Further inquiry soon revealed that someone had pulled out the power plug from a concentrator box for the eight screens (to plug in an electric typewriter – the ultimate irony!). Another end user reported a system crash, without checking with her supervisor or even looking at CPU, disk drives or printers. It transpired that her terminal had blanked out when a boy-friend sat on her desk to talk to her and inadvertently nudged the on-off switch
– treat electronic mail and messaging as the same thing; they aren't
– tell anyone your system is idiot-proof; aside from flouting the 28 laws of Murphy, you've no idea what *intelligent* idiots can get up to!

5

Organizational implications

Demonstrating an operational need for word processing and implementing suitable solutions to fulfil that requirement are only part of the overall corporate picture. The costs of doing it must be justified.

The costs of installing advanced WP systems in purely hardware and software terms are unlikely to be trivial. On the other hand, as hardware costs decline and software becomes increasingly structured and modular, there is already in sight a 'crossover' point where WP systems will be at least as cheap as the complex electro-mechanical machines they replace.

The cost differential for an electronic, limited-memory typewriter is already slim in both directions – down to mechanical and standard electrics and up to stand-alone WP. The lowest-specification electronic correcting typewriters were already priced lower than the best correcting-ribbon electro-mechanical machine by 1982. Typewriters will not last for ever, and must be replaced – why not by WP systems costing much the same while potentially needing less human effort, both at the keyboard and for maintenance?

There is also the important question as to whether any organization can afford the cost of *not* converting to WP; which brings us on to the less than directly quantifiable benefits and possible costs of widespread conversion to WP for corporate text production.

What is better document (and arguably information) *quality* worth to an organization? How will working conditions, patterns, performance and organizational structures be affected? How can these effects be optimally controlled?

This section addresses these questions, after looking at the need for a methodology to address the quantitative and qualitative cost/benefit analysis of the effects of introducing WP.

It also looks in overview at the important question of security, in terms of both privacy and integrity of information. The security issue has always existed with paper-based text handling but appears to be given significant additional poignancy in most people's minds by the prospect of systems whose ultimate function must be to make all corporate knowledge at least theoretically available at each and every work-station.

5.1 COST/BENEFIT AND EFFECTIVENESS ANALYSES

Justifying the investment in new systems must be an ongoing process, starting as a theoretical activity to warrant the budgetary commitment and carrying through to retroactive appraisal of the benefits and costs of actual running, both predicted and unexpected. Costs and benefits can be established at every level of visibility, ranging from the uncontradictably demonstrable to the hypothetically perceptible.

This section details the ways in which the provable may be measured and the possible postulated. It offers a set of guidelines on the basis of which it should be possible for any organization to elaborate, and over a period of years fine-tune, a methodology for establishing with locally specific accuracy the likely direct effects of introducing new technology, with a fair stab at the less concrete results.

5.1.1 Capital and running costs

The *capital* costs of installing new systems ought to be relatively easy to calculate, consisting chiefly of:

– site preparation electrical work
communications
building alterations
re-decoration

	sound-proofing (possible)
	air conditioning (if necessary)
	fire/flood precautions
– furnishing	special-purpose desks/tables anti-static carpeting
– equipment	as specified and priced by supplier
– media	start-up supplies of recording media, magnetic and paper; may be included in equipment price
– cables	usually (but not always) included in equipment price
– training	usually bundled into the equipment supply price
– delivery	also usually included by supplier
– software	packages purchased rather than hired or included in the global system supply price
– relocation	(possibly) of staff to make room for central equipment and/or storage space, air conditioning machinery

There is also the debatable question as to whether the costs of time, direct expenses and indirect overheads of staff engaged on pre-implementation studies and actual installation should be counted as a one-off project cost and capitalized as such.

Running costs represent something of a grey area, in which the best-considered forward estimates can go substantially astray when a system is actually installed. This is due in no small part to typical surges in throughput due to (a) taking up suppressed demand, and (b) newly-found ability to re-draft documents easily.

Elements of running cost which need to be taken into account will include:

– systems support	hardware maintenance
	software support
	development activity
	cleaning (gentle)
– power supply	cost increases, especially if, for example, a CPU is kept running round the clock (a recommendable practice for large systems) or air cooling is involved

– consumables	disks print ribbons/ink/toner print heads/wheels paper (probably a lot more).

5.1.2 Indirect/hidden costs

A number of indirect costs will be associated with the installation and running of any new system. Some of these will be apparent well in advance of implementation, others will be less predictable and the degree to which they occur or not will be very organization-specific.

Such items may include:

- staff demands for increased payment for WP-based work. This can be resisted (but has sometimes been volunteered as a path-smoothing introductory gesture) by management as far as extra effort or skills are concerned, since WP demonstrably makes life easier for the typist. But if the argument is based on 'speed-up' (i.e. substantial increase in throughput) it may be difficult not to concede the point
- hiring costs of WP-experienced supervisory personnel
- severance pay for personnel rendered redundant by the introduction of WP systems. Experience among large WP users has usually been, however, that natural wastage is high and rapid enough among typing staff (especially in large cities) that, when it is combined with some redeployment severance costs can be largely avoided
- authors will take excessive advantage of the new facilities and demand, for example, multiple re-drafts of documents which they would have previously been glad to approve after only one corrective pass. This hidden addition to the basic workload may be desirable (since arguably better-finished output results), but must be taken into account in looking at the true costs of a new system
- work from sections and departments not yet equipped with advanced WP facilities is often (usually rapidly and somewhat clandestinely) transferred to any new system, completely distorting the before-and-after picture. Again, this may well be a corporate benefit in operational terms, but it must be counted as a distinct burden on the new system when calculating its real cost-effectiveness

- some end users may feel de-skilled by the use of powerful new systems, which remove the need (and motivation) for constant attention to accuracy and details of document layout; their keyboarding performance may drop off and disenchantment spread to a complete work section. The worst of this effect is usually found where boring, repetitive document production is considered (e.g. invoice typing) and can be overcome by giving the end user a varied selection of more interesting work
- the new-found ability to correct any mistake with ease can induce a degree of relaxation amounting to sloppiness in copy typing. End users then tend to treat everything as a rough first draft, which can cost a considerable amount of (a) indirect user effort in correcting errors, and (b) additional direct user work in editing out those errors. An effective antidote exists: supervisors should ensure that end users are responsible for the quality of a document throughout its production life, i.e. the typist who makes an error must also correct it; this tends to decrease the error count quite drastically
- the introduction of new information processing technology can have quite deep, and lasting effects on an organization's work patterns and overall structure (see sections 5.2 and 5.3). In any environment where the user labour is organized, this will naturally have repercussions on industrial relations, consuming considerable amounts of management time in negotiation
- suppliers usually charge extra for training staff who may eventually replace the original batch who were given instruction as part of the original system supply package. If the organization decides to train its own trainers, this in itself will also represent an additional ongoing source of costs. Even with a highly stable complement of staff, with little turnover from one year to the next, training in the use of new software releases and add-on facilities will cost a calculable (but unfortunately not easily predictable) amount.

5.1.3 Directly quantifiable benefits

Most benefits which can be accurately quantified will be expressed in terms of cost *savings* produced by introducing WP. These will include (but be far from limited to):

- end user time and effort. Experience indicates that secretarial typing productivity will be enhanced by between 60 and 80 per cent by the use of an advanced word processor, properly managed pool/copy typing by anywhere between 125 per cent and a quite staggering 700 per cent (for very heavy multiple drafts with substantial changes between drafts)
- indirect user time in checking text after the first draft; once captured correctly in electronic form, text stays correct and never needs re-keying, with its inherent risk of second-pass error
- elimination of conventional typing machine costs; as the cost of electronic word processing equipment approaches that of conventional electro-mechanical machines, this represents a substantial offset to the purchase of WP systems
- possible overall reduction in maintenance costs. A support contract for WP systems will typically cost between 10 per cent and 15 per cent of system price, of which between 5 per cent and 7 per cent will probably be attributable to hardware maintenance. The annual cost of maintaining electro-mechanical typing hardware is now of the order of 25 per cent of its purchase price.
- elimination of corrective medium costs: correction fluids, papers (Tipp-Ex, etc.) and ribbons (e.g. IBM lift-off tape); in the early 1980s, these costs were far from trivial in conventional typing environments
- if a typesetting interface is available/developed or a variable typefount printer selected (see section 6) all preparation costs (re-keying and page layout) of producing typeset-quality documents is eliminated. As these constitute the major element of cost in printing (and reprographic and binding work will have to be done with either method), the differential cost of high-quality reproduction may be eliminated
- if a decision is made to archive documentation centrally in magnetic or optical form (microfiche output or optical disk – see section 6), *very* considerable amounts of storage space used for paper documentation may be liberated. While this saving may be more notional than actual in an existing building, where a new building is concerned, it may make a very considerable contribution to the cost of the new system, simply by eliminating the cost of constructing, decorating and furnishing a corporate archive. In one large administrative author-

ity, for example, saving 500 square metres of central registry space was estimated as reducing by £70,000 to £100,000 the cost of its new building

- if the potential of a large-scale implementation of WP is used to the full, head-count trimming could reduce significantly the amount of space required for people. Alternatively, using communications facilities to facilitate distribution of typing effort to remote locations can very substantially reduce the bill for real estate. It costs between 10 and 15 times as much to house a copy typist in central London, for example, as 25–30 miles away in practically any direction.

5.1.4 Semi-quantifiable benefits

These are, almost by definition, more likely to be found in areas relating to indirect usage of new systems, and many will relate to generation of new sales revenue as opposed to saving costs. Solid and demonstrable, but perhaps difficult to put a precise monthly figure on, these benefits will include:

- greater impact on the prospective customer, especially with customized mail-shots. One large supplier in the electronics industry measured an increase in the 'hit rate' (qualified sales prospects likely to buy something) achieved by promotional mailing to pre-qualified 'suspects' (those who might respond) from around four in a hundred to eleven per cent within weeks of introducing a powerful new semi-standard letter facility
- accelerated handling of sales transactions from first contact to final invoice, leading to general advancement of cash inflow
- more effective pursuit of tardy or defaulting debtors
- faster support of sales personnel in the field, greater ability to follow-up sales leads quickly and fully, meaning better conversion rate for leads into sales
- reduced overall cost of marketing activities, including the release of personnel tied up by document production to sell more directly
- general saving in wasted management time and effort. Probably the most immediate (and almost directly quantifiable) saving in this area may be achieved with telephone systems, using the people-tracking potential of a computerized switchboard to the full – but this is outside the scope of this book

and warrants a tome all to itself. However, the *combined* potential in this respect of communicating word processors and the SPC/PABX (stored-program controlled private automatic branch exchange) is considerable, for example, in collaborative authorship of large documents or pre-discussion transfer of relevant documents.

5.1.5 Qualitative enhancement

When looking at the management benefits of new information handling systems, this is undoubtedly one of the more difficult areas.

Most managers will accept that better information systems will deliver better all-round performance, but judgment on both these matters will always be highly subjective. It will never, for example, be possible conclusively to *prove* that better information results in better decisions, meaning better business performance. But a historical perspective drawn over a period of years will support the strong probability that these matters are very directly linked.

In preparing a strong case for the introduction of any information system it *must* be recognized that the intangibles will almost certainly constitute far and away the most convincing long-term justification for the present commitment of funds. Some of the areas worth pointing up and detailing in making such a case will include:

- better *quality* of information support: manifested in faster delivery, fuller coverage, and a greater certainty on the part of the user of that information that he/she is (a) looking at an accurate statement, and (b) not missing any vital part of the corporate store of knowledge. Word processing, as the key element of capture and possibly a vital part of presentation of synopses, is very germane to the issue of quality.
- more time to make decisions: always provided that the extra time to meet decision-making deadlines which WP and office automation can undoubtedly deliver is used to give the decider more time to think and relax, rather than (as many fear) simply putting more pressure on fewer people to make more decisions in even less time
- corporate document quality (and hence image): reflected in better presented documentation ranging from simple acknowledgement notes to hefty user manuals
- better quality of recruited staff: attracted by a corporate

image of advanced working environments, allied to faster and better-presented processing of job applications, at the first contact stage with prospective employees (the recruitment process is itself one application area certain to benefit from end user saving in WP, as identified in section 5.1.2)

– reduced turnover of existing good staff: a strong tendency is discernible for good staff to stay with a company not just for money, but because of the quality of its working environment and overall image. (This again can result in directly quantifiable savings in hiring fees, reduced loss of executive time while new recruits are brought up to corporate speed.)

– generally perceived enhancement in the quality of working life, including reduced strain on senior executives. (This has also been known to effect direct savings in sickness and – in extreme pressure areas – death benefits, often allied to consequent new hiring costs.)

5.2 CHANGING WORK-PATTERNS

In any office environment, from fast-moving sales support to humdrum local government, the advent of powerful word processors will effect quite major changes in working patterns, methods, procedures and styles. Some of these may be quite immediate, others will evolve as knowledge grows among users – both direct and indirect – of the different ways in which WP techniques can be used to improve performance. Not all users will necessarily welcome that change. There will always be some who fear change because they are afraid they cannot adapt. Still more who may yet find it difficult to accept what appears to be the cardinal precept of the microchip revolution, that the only constant is change itself. Change must therefore be closely monitored and tightly managed.

This section looks at some of the ways in which recent experience indicates change will manifest itself in terms of work patterns, and suggests some of the methods which have helped to derive optimal benefit from its processes (so far, that is – it could all be changing right now!).

5.2.1 Involving those involved

Only the unprepared find change problematical. If everyone who is to be associated with a major change in ways of working is involved to some degree in specifying the nature and extent of that change, then there should be no nasty surprises. This is particularly important with word processing since, as indicated elsewhere in this book, the majority of system suppliers still see users being adapted to fit the capabilities of the system they are selling rather than vice versa, as it ought to be.

If direct end users (typists and those who supervise them) are involved in discussion from the start of any automation project and – since they are the real experts – their considered advice is well taken by the planners, the system specification developed in-house will fairly tightly constrain the choice of supplier and the design of the system he supplies. Provided that indirect users (authors and decision-makers) are equally closely involved, it is unlikely that the system will either address serious tasks incompetently or overkill trivia.

Discussion groups, possibly involving both direct and indirect users together occasionally (but not often, since their overviews will differ substantially) should be established as soon as possible after the decision is taken formally to launch a word processing project. These groups will later evolve conveniently into user groups which can then turn their attention to the fine-tuning and development of the system(s) installed. The group chairman should always be a senior member of the project management team, to give continuing directional thrust and make final decisions where issues may not emerge as clear-cut. It will be useful, and practical in terms of using time to the best advantage, to integrate user familiarization with the building and growth of these discussion groups.

Working demonstrations, the showing of videotapes and films, and occasional attendance of representatives from organizations already committed to advanced WP should help promote well targetted discussion, and make all attendees increasingly comfortable with the prospect of change.

Nearer to system procurement time, it will be very helpful if a small group of end users, possibly not more than two or three, can be given early hands-on exposure to the various types of system hardware and software on the project short-list, and spend some time feeding back their impressions, objections and suggestions to the project management team. This reaction should be quickly synthesized into a review of changes required from the various suppliers, and will make a significant contribution to the overall process of evaluation.

As remarked elsewhere in this book (and it is hard to overstress the importance of the point) the best system in the world will not perform brilliantly if its users don't like it. Conversely, seemingly awkward and inadequate systems have proved very effective in the hands of intelligent users who liked some of the functions and shaped other system facilities to meet their own needs.

5.2.2 Work flow patterns and creative style

The introduction of WP can significantly affect the patterns of work in any organization. Peaks and troughs of work can be quickly flattened to provide a smoother rhythm of throughput, partly since many peaks in office word handling are attributable to fairly predictable monthly 'crisis-points' in, for example, report production.

WP allows pre-preparation of substantial amounts of new material for integration into final reports and, perhaps more importantly, can be used to retrieve and reproduce necessary detail from previous periods. A classic example is the rolling 12-month financial operating statement used by many organizations, where only one column of figures is actually new, but the rest all need to be moved left (or right) and one column deleted (an important role for good tabular format control).

The extra power per work-station of WP also lends itself well to absorbing panic sessions of unpredictable load. Where work-stations are linked to central units or network among themselves, sudden heavy input loads can also be evenly spread over a well-managed integrated system.

Text production against very tight deadlines can be completely revolutionized by using WP. A good example on the marketing front can be seen with the preparation of often massive, highly technical proposals in the electronics industry. With conventional typing, such proposals would take an inordinate time, and often result in an unsightly mixture of different typefaces and pre-printed materials. Perhaps more significantly, if a sales executive discovered only a week before proposal delivery date that he was actually on the wrong tack, changing the proposal and the key management summary parts of it were next to impossible. With WP, the whole volume can be re-wrought in 48 hours, and with the advanced print devices now coming into use, no problems with lead time for typeset-quality printing rear their heads at the last minute.

This ability to re-work documentation up to the last possible minute (even while the first few pages are already being run off on the printer) is a great boon to all creative writing effort. Authors now have the option to experiment with various presentations, both in content and format, before committing themselves.

Scheduling of the author's time for other activity is also made much more flexible, since (as noted above) WP enables documentation to be systematically prepared sectionally in advance and then run together, while lost time can easily be caught up with an intensive, but mercifully short, typing session.

As we have already seen, WP systems also make audio typing much less of a painful drudgery for the typist, and iterative audio/draft correction processes between author and amanuensis are on the increase. This process will be further streamlined (and already has in many places) by the practice of authors with limited keyboard skills using simplified editing tools to correct bulk text input by a typing expert.

Some authors will also develop skills in using the WP terminal much more directly, for origination of many documents. While executives have traditionally resisted direct keyboarding themselves, the emergence of simpler interfaces and radically new keying concepts could change this quite dramatically. It may well be significant (and certainly instructive) in this respect that 75 per cent of the executives of one major quasi-governmental organization formed during the 1970s expressed a willingness (and showed some talent) for direct use of typing keyboards. They were all youngish people, had been grouped together to form a dynamic energy-industry concern in short order, and were desperate for typing support in a large city short of high-quality secretarial assistance.

A few users (including the author of this book, an ex-journalist with a background of three-finger typing) have reached the point where they can no longer create structured text without a keyboard under their practised (albeit still inexpert!) fingers and a screen to look at when the fingers know they have done something wrong, or the layout needs prettying up. It may yet be some time before all those who could usefully achieve this level of plug-compatible humanity actually do so. But the principal psychological barriers to doing so are already down, due in very large part to the increasing mass use by all members of any workforce of personal, home and games computers, removing many of the cultural myths and quasi-taboos about using keyboards and screens. Moreover, many executives already interface fairly directly to the corporate computer system for information retrieval and quite advanced presentational use of computer graphics. Most of them will, for quite a high percentage of this work, find it useful to integrate short passages of explanatory text with numbers and pictures. How much longer before they key in their own supporting text?

5.2.3 Cutting down paperwork

If managers make use of keyboards and screens to create pictures, text and number tables – and many already do – there will soon come a point when they begin to ask whether a paper record is absolutely necessary to transfer that information to their colleagues. Why not enter that data into the corporate information store, and let those needing to use it (and authorized to do so) retrieve it when and how they want? Technically, there is every reason why they should; but culturally, it may take a little longer to accept that paper is not an essential recording medium. Cheap, freely available paper storage has been with us roughly the same length of time that 'the office' has meant the paper factory and not the job worked at, and everyone now working in offices is familiar with the paper mountain.

Historically, there has been a good rationale for paper being chosen over other computer recording media such as magnetic tape, disk or microfilm. Paper was cheap, easily available, portable, durable, showed up alterations and all but the best forgeries, was freely interchangeable between organizations having different business systems and legally acceptable for archival purposes. With the microprocessor revolution, things are changing quite dramatically.

For a start, paper is no longer cheap, and it has for some time been much more economical to store three or four magnetic versions of a document than two copies on A4 bond paper. With the advent of optical disks, that disparity in cost will be magnified by a factor of 10,000 or more. While paper is still easily available, it is a gradually vanishing world resource, with forests unable to keep pace with pulping mills. A leading science fiction writer who is no mean mathematician estimated around 1970 that, by about AD 2040, the weight of documentary paper in the world would equal the weight of the world. Not unreasonably, he concluded that something would have to change in the way humanity records its transactions and thought processes.

Meanwhile, back in the real world, over the decade 1970–1980, most large merchant banks proved his point by quadrupling their holding of paper files *despite* heavy introduction of computerized information processing. In the 1990s, paper will be neither cheap nor, perhaps, (at least without major recycling effort and the incorporation of new raw materials) so freely available.

As regards portability, computer media already have a comfortable edge; even a lightly packed floppy disk can carry 100 pages of A4 which would outweigh it and its cover by at least five or six times. Optical disks will enable users to carry around whole van-loads of equivalent paper text under one lightly loaded arm.

Durability is no problem with optical (microfilm or optical disk) output from computers – they are much more durable than paper. Even magnetic disks and tape, properly 'exercised' at intervals, have a shelf life of at least five years.

While magnetic recordings can be altered, (a) this is not possible without physical access to a machine as well as the recording medium, (b) any computer system record can be given a better level of security protection than a paper file, and (c) computers can be programmed to back-track to the forger. As regards optical media they are more ineradicable than paper.

Interchangeability of information in computer-generated form will continue to be something more of a problem until established standards for inter-communication are agreed by suppliers. Nonetheless, many organizations already conduct substantial electronic interchange (direct funds transfer for example) and document scanner-digitizers will make it all much more feasible, even with handwritten originals.

Finally, legal acceptance of computer records has been slow, chiefly because of doubts about the longevity of magnetic recordings and the potential for alteration or eradication. However, the courts of many countries now accept microform recordings (although their validity must usually be attested to on paper by an independent witness), and optical disks seem likely to be even more acceptable.

Despite the opportunities for streamlining exchange offered by electronics, it will probably still be a long while before the flow of paper in offices is reduced, let alone extinguished. The author of this book used to lecture from time to time on the 'paperless office'. Experience having demonstrated that this was not an immediately acceptable prospect, he altered that to read 'less-paper office'. Extensive experience of WP implementation of WP having demonstrated that less paper was the last thing users of WP were looking for initially and paper flow actually tended to *in*crease for at least the first few months, the title was changed to the less controversial 'Office of the future' (arguably all things to all men).

There is still very much the feeling in most organizations that information somehow only really counts when recorded on paper; this cultural sensibility will take a while to dissolve.

There is also the potential danger of electronic junk mail: the computer allows a user to inundate his reading public with far greater masses of largely useless information than any paper system ever could. There is, however, already practical implementation of a most promising kind. One large oil company, deciding that the best way to make business decisions was to put its major decision-makers in direct touch with real-time data, paid out over a million pounds to produce a splendid system for its 29 top executives. They have a full-colour terminal enabling them to access 36 major corporate databases, and present or extrapolate that data in many ways. Given that a decision by any one of the 29 can be worth several million pounds at a time, the expenditure is well worth it. That way lies the route to optimal use of computer-held information: synthesis of information in all its forms in a way that highly experienced users can grasp simply and immediately.

5.3 NEW STAFFING STRUCTURES

The introduction of modern WP systems opens up opportunities for structural improvement in several areas of the middle-to large-sized organization, and will virtually demand some change in *any* size or type of enterprise. As the first element of the integrated office information handling system of the future, it paves the way for much more direct access to information by the users of information. In its more advanced forms, it will also demand different and enhanced skills from staff associated with the handling of words.

Perhaps the greatest opportunity computer-based WP presents to any organization, when coupled with communications, lies with the ability to associate text production capacity very directly with the functions which need it, while not being tied to any specific physical location. The ultimate distributed WP configuration could very well be seen in 'cottaging' – working from home or close to it.

This section looks at the structural opportunities and organizational needs involved in taking the best advantage of advanced WP.

5.3.1 Distribution of WP support functions

Large central typing pool operations have rarely proved wholly satisfactory, except for rather specialized functions in narrowly oriented service departments of large organizations. The attractions of staffing flexibility are often outweighed by the difficulties of managing very large numbers of people serving a multiplicity of different needs, and by the grinding impersonality of the whole arrangement. Conversely, attempts to manage centrally the activity of secretarial typists have usually run into trouble due to the sheer complexity of the management task in controlling personnel at widely separated physical locations.

Communicating word processors open up a number of new possibilities of operating a form of hybrid system where central management can be quite strong, while physical distance between work-station users is virtually irrelevant. The workload status of machines connected to a central network can be easily examined at any point in time, leaving the WP manager free to send work (e.g. audio tapes, either physically or using the house telephone as a link) to lightly loaded stations to help in balancing overall levels of throughput. Most of the time, therefore, any given typist or small typing section can be physically located conveniently close to the executive function principally served, while still being available for overload shifting. In this situation, too, having a work-station or two temporarily out of service need cause no great problems; the work is simply moved elsewhere until the fault is cleared. Alternatively, typing staff can be grouped more together, in cheaper-cost sites physically remote from the various departments they serve, but kept in close operational (and social) contact by the telephone and text transmission network.

5.3.2 Working from home

Perhaps the ultimate level of distribution for an office system may come with individuals working most of the time from home, or at least a communications equipped centre much closer to their homes than the office building where they would normally have worked. This has already been done with conventional typewriters by one large insurance company, somewhat physically cut off from the rest of the UK and wanting to hold on to its best typing talent even after the ladies concerned left work to become housewives and mothers. The company organized a small team of part-time typists from recent leavers, supplied them with standard electric typewriters, and paid them piecework rates for copy-typing documents whose original drafts were sent to them at home. A motor-cycle courier distributed input and collected output on a daily round and the 'cottaging' staff were left, within fairly broad limits, to schedule their own work.

All this becomes a lot easier with communicating word processors and, given the rapidly increasing portability of competent WP terminals, and the fact that any home can now have an excellent telecommunications link (the phone) there are obviously some promising opportunities to use time more efficiently here.

Apart from making the working life of skilled individuals much more attractive, cottaging plus communications can have immediate financial benefits for a large organization. Using the homes of employees who do not actually need to be centrally gathered and are capable of some self-management, cottaging can save substantial real-estate costs. Since quite a high percentage of office employee earnings in metropolitan areas normally goes straight out again in travel expenses, a significantly reduced need to commute will be attractive to the cottaging worker. Organizations will also be able, using such techniques, to pick and choose the best text handling workers from a very wide geographical catchment area.

It may well be, of course, that social problems will delay or even debar such a move. Many workers probably need the atmosphere change from home to office to get the best out of them, some will not work well without direct management control, while many will feel the need to work alongside others.

The local work-centre, linked by high-capacity wideband circuits to central computer resources may well be a credible alternative, so that employees can work close to home rather than in it. But in either case, and especially in megalopolitan areas where skilled staff are at a premiium and commuting is tediously expensive, the traditional office environment could well be on its way out for the great bulk of information-handling staff.

5.3.3 The information scientists

In order to cope with the constantly increasing flow of information within an organization, and to enable its value to be fully realized, new skills and disciplines will be needed among support staff.

First will come the WP system supervisors, learning and teaching the new techniques and procedures associated with computer-supported working, managing and throughput of textual information, and acting as the first line of system trouble-shooter. Next will be communications controllers, with a broad technical base in telecommunications but, much more importantly, an ability to analyse and design systems to support the way that human individuals communicate among themselves. Not a few of the half-forgotten arts of operational research will be needed here. Then will come an entirely new breed of super-librarian, specializing in the design and implementation of electronic registries and providing user-friendly retrieval facilities for non-specialist users.

These facilities may well, for some time to come, be provided largely by the information scientist carrying out searches through a powerful information database system on behalf of the non-technical inquirer. Later, more directly user-driven query languages and semi-expert sub-systems may begin to take over (but that is for another time and perhaps another book!).

One very important sub-species of the new breed of information scientist will be the super-secretary, now turned electronic archivist, and probably doing very little of the typing which was so important to the executive(s) with whom she once worked. Keyboarding was, after all, only an important skill when it was difficult to get right, and when observance of house rules was an intellectual exercise rather than a function of the typing machine.

Sitting on top of all this new science must come the team of strategic planners, headed by an individual or small group of individuals with a wide spectrum of skills and operational background, to design, support and keep enhancing the integrated office of the future (see section 6.3).

5.3.4 Management information systems

The ultimate, central aim of the electronic office must be to support more effectively the work of the people it is designed to support. For executives, the need is to come to closer grips with up-to-date, accurate information, properly presented and thoroughly researched.

The effect of new, integrated information management systems, in which WP and text retrieval will play key roles, will be to make information much more directly accessible to decision-makers, while at the same time enhancing the role of those who manage the support systems capturing and presenting that information. The likely structural effect – already visible in some more dynamically changing organizations – will be to flatten the corporate structure considerably, and broaden somewhat the apex of the traditional pyramid at its secondary layer. A whole middle stratum of the pyramid will be squeezed and could be eliminated – the junior and middle executive layer traditionally filtering (some would say impeding) and communicating directives down to the ground floor and interpreting responses on their way up to the boardroom. If senior management can get the information they want direct from computer systems supported by knowledgeable information scientists, the need for the communicating layer disappears. Many types of organization may also see a general erosion of the differential between director and directed, with an evolution more towards a shared-responsibility concept of planners and executors.

5.4 INFORMATION SECURITY

As more and more corporate knowledge is captured and stored electronically, the user organization becomes progressively more dependent on the ready availability of that information. With new and more sophisticated electronic mechanisms being devised to interpret and synthesize that information, dependence will also increasingly reflect operational vulnerability to system failure, penetration by outsiders able to make use of its contents, or even fraudulent misuse by insiders.

Any piece of information is at risk once it is communicated beyond its originator, and total protection of any recorded knowledge from accident or attack must be either impossibly difficult or prohibitively expensive, and quite possibly both.

In designing mechanisms to safeguard the integrity of corporate information, and keeping it from prying eyes, protective expenditure must be balanced very directly against the value of the information. If its destruction or dissemination would cause business collapse, then quite elaborate and costly precautions are obviously justified. If minor embarrassment and a lot of remedial work will be the only upshot, then obviously the security sights can be set a lot lower.

This section looks at 'security' in its three major meanings: integrity of information, confidentiality and physical system protection. A fourth sense of the word is emerging in many fast-working organizations which needs also to be remembered in relevant system design: an assurance that information available at any work-station in the corporate system is fully updated, with the facility to ask what today's business situation is and get a *very* precise and immediate answer.

5.4.1 Integrity

Users who rely on information based systems must be sure that the information base is reliable, accurate and cannot be lost, or accidentally corrupted. This has a number of implications for system managers including:

- copies of all working electronic files must be maintained at all times. Ideally, WP practices will borrow from those already established in DP and keep up the grandfather, father, son hierarchy of copies, with the son being the currently on-line version of the files). This means rigorous, routine and frequent copying of working disks and/or tapes, and (again ideally) the maintenance of a grandfather copy away from the immediate vicinity of the work-station(s) involved, so that a lost or corrupt set of files can be reconstituted quickly with only recent updates missing
- procedures must be established to ensure that backup copies of electronically held files are never mounted on a suspected faulty system until the fault has been positively cleared
- communications between systems or in a network must be rigorously monitored for possible data corruption in transit. This implies data block and parity checks beyond the scope of this book, but well known to any network designer
- access to systems must be strictly controlled, and authorization to modify important files even more so. Ideally, a mechanism should be incorporated into a corporate file-handling system such that only authorized users can modify files, others can only read them
- ready availability of information for all users should be guaranteed by having sufficient backup equipment to cope reasonably well with any local failure
- large sub-systems shared by many terminals must be duplicated, ideally in separate physical locations
- system software should have inbuilt checks so that when files are transferred or copied from one medium to another the copy exactly matches the original.

5.4.2 Confidentiality

Levels of protection against unauthorized access to corporate information stores will vary sharply from organization to organization, starting at the top with the defence establishment.

Paper systems were always vulnerable, but somehow many people refuse to believe that computers can be made at least as secure from intrusion as a book in a safe with a combination lock. In fact, given a reasonably competent operating system and file-handling mechanism, they can be made a great deal safer.

Multiple logical locks can be built into file handlers on even quite modestly priced word processors, effectively able to restrict access to a specific file to a named individual using a combination of two or more changeable passwords and a terminal user code (for example). Access can be further restricted to read-only, modify in part or whole, transmit part/whole and delete part/whole. For the more worried user, back-tracking system logs can establish who tried to break the system and blow loud warning whistles (literally or metaphorically) if attempted intrusion is detected taking place. Logical barriers can be heavily reinforced by physical work-station locks, magnetic badge readers or even fingerprint scanners, all, of course, at an appropriate level of cost.

Provided that a user organization can guarantee (or obtain such guarantee from its supplier) that no system user or support personnel can interfere with the operating system (and these are fairly well locked up in this day and age) it is quite difficult even to perpetrate an 'inside job'.

All this refers to documentation in electronic form, and it is worth noting that (a) WP systems are at their most vulnerable when printing out information onto paper, and (b) the great majority of confidentiality violations are down to accidental loss (leaving paper about in most cases).

Paper distribution systems need to be carefully monitored and, in a highly secure environment, single-pass print ribbons and carbon paper should be destroyed along with any paper copies consigned for shredding. An expert can read a carbon ribbon almost as fast as the characters were keyed; it needs no expert to read a one-pass sheet of carbon.

Text is also vulnerable to intrusion while in transmission from place to place, either locally at a site or in wider-area transit. For the local site, fibre-optic cable can make it difficult for an intruder to tap into a signal stream and impossible to do so undetected (the tapping-in distorts the optical characteristics of the fibre and hence its signal-passing qualities, causing data corruption and (usually) triggering alarms. But the most effective way to deter an intruder when *any* physical communications medium is used is to encrypt the data, using a microchip-based descendant of the original military 'scrambler' telephone device.

5.4.3 Site protection

Sensitive work areas (e.g. personnel departments internally, marketing externally) need some degree of physical protection for their WP systems against access or damage by intruders. Large centrally shared units (e.g. laser printers, big disk units) need more safeguards.

Site security can vary considerably, between the odd closed-circuit TV camera mounted in the reception lobby to an encircling 20-foot deep corridor prowled 24 hours a day by killer dogs (an actual practice in one, non-military, European DP centre). Somewhere in between these extremes will be the right balance of protection-system cost to protected-item value to suit each individual organization.

Options for restricting access to all or part of sensitive sites will include:

- numeric-combination keypad electronic locks (cheap but usually ineffectual, tend to keep out authorized staff with poor memories rather than observant intruders with good ones)
- magnetic-stripe badge readers for secure areas (reasonably priced, and can often be integrated with flexitime clocks)
- fingerprint or voice recognition door-locks (expensive but certain)
- window, door and skylight alarms (individual noise-makers or silent alarm triggering)
- vibration sensors to detect drilling/hammering into floor, wall or ceiling drilling
- lift lobby CCTV monitors, possibly combined with physical or magnetic locks to keep unauthorized lift users from reaching sensitive work-floors.

6

From word processor to electronic office

6.1 WP AT THE CENTRE OF THE OFFICE OF THE FUTURE

Word processing has achieved the same kind of industrial revolution in the office as the Jacquard loom control system in textile factories. Left as a stand-alone solution, however, WP is achieving for the user only a fraction of what it might.

Better production of paper documentation, in terms of output capacity, accuracy and presentation, is undoubtedly important. But paper-held information is, with assistance from the so-called convenience copier, inevitably unwieldy to manipulate and frequently difficult to retrieve in immediately meaningful shape. And WP techniques, while demonstrably effective in reducing the cost of paper document production, only address a very small fraction – typically less than five per cent – of all office information-handling costs.

Optimally implemented, a major word processing installation will do well if it cuts typing costs in half; as typing accounts for only some 10 per cent of office expenses, with over 40 per cent down to management and professionals, WP is simply not doing enough if it only outputs paper-held text.

It is only when we come to look at the potential of widespread use of WP for capture of information in electronic form that we can see not only the ultimate potential for WP systems in information handling, but the very essential nature of WP at the centre of the electronic office of the future.

It has been estimated that an 'average' office day (always supposing that either can be averaged) will see the output of something like 10 ethnic words (or about 70 bytes of computer disk space) for every 10 bytes of numeric data. Until the mid-1970s, most offices captured words on paper and data in some electro-magnetic form so that virtually all electronic information was numeric.

But, with the increasing use, power and general sophistication of text-handling systems, electronic capture is increasingly on the side of text, while at the same time the distinction between text and data is progressively blurred and merged – as perhaps it should have always have been – in the overall flow of *information* processing. As technology progresses, this integrated handling of information will expand to embrace information in all its forms – text, data, graphics and voice – and the truly integrated 'office system' will be here.

The advance towards integration has been gradual, however, and may be expected to be a relatively slow progress, held back mainly by innate human resistance to both sudden change and the discipline of tightly imposed standards necessary to achieve the eventual freedom of an open systems architecture in which all types of information handling system or sub-system can be simply inter-connected.

6.2 IN-HOUSE, TYPESET-QUALITY PRINTING

A first, and, in many organizations, most important, step to expand the potential for advanced WP is into the simple production of documentation of a quality hitherto expected from the printing press rather than the typewriter.

Many print shops have already switched largely from press to photocopier for production of limited print runs of high-quality documentation. It has been obvious for several years that very large, computer-linked laser printers could outperform in flexibility and print quality all but the largest and most expensive of their phototypesetting/copying cousins.

Advanced technology has brought together microprocessor power and economy with the flexibility of control of lasers and light-emitting diode (LED) matrices to the point where, for the next generation of office systems, the distinction between printer and photosetter will become academic. Already, intelligent laser and LED printers able to store and reproduce a great multiplicity of print styles have come down from the half-million dollar level unthinkable for all but the heaviest users to around $US 20,000. The technology is such that market forces will probably drive these prices down below $10,000 in very short order: in mid-1983 one small US supplier was already offering a multi-fount desktop laser printer from $4,000.

While laser and LED printers have made very rapid technical strides, medium-speed needle-matrix impact printers have also been bridging the gap, from legible imprint to attractive typefount, which ruled out their use for all but drafting purposes with the first generation of word processing systems. Using double matrices, with as many as 18 needles overstriking and infilling, combined with microprocessor output control and stored typefounts, matrix printers can now emulate the traditional daisy-wheel and come close to typesetters for quality. They can, moreover, do it in colour and provide carbon copies if required, neither of which a laser printer can do.

A word processing system properly interfaced to one (or more) of these new multi-fount machines, and ideally sharing its/their speed and flexibility with a number of other text capture devices, effectively eliminates the traditional need for double-keying of text to achieve typeset-quality. It also makes it possible to address a very large in-house printing need which has not been catered for since the obsolescence of IBM's magnetic-tape-based composer-typewriter systems.

Virtually any existing typefount can be digitized in a few man-days' work at most and stored in the memory of the new generation of smart printers. The opportunity is also now wide open for custom design of individual house type-styles over and above the rather limited range which the average jobbing printer has traditionally offered. For international organizations, the way is now open to using a complete range of national typefaces, interchangeably with the same printer addressed from national or hybrid keyboards. To take full advantage of the new printer possibilities, it will be desirable to develop print control boxes (or servers) which can handle a wide variety of hardware devices, act as input buffering storage devices and provide a wide range of type styles to be selected on-line by the outputting WP device.

6.3 COMMUNICATING TEXT: 'ELECTRONIC MAIL'

The phrase 'electronic mail' has found probably more interpretations even than the liberally misused 'word processing', covering a wide spectrum of techniques and technological options. It is, indeed, only recently that distinction has increasingly been made between mail, or the not usually time-critical communication of complete documents and 'messaging', i.e. relatively urgent transmission of short textual items. For the longer term, it will be necessary to define the 'document' more completely than hitherto, to cover all forms of information transmission.

A suggested definition would run: 'information in textual, numeric, voice or graphical form of which there is a lasting, structured record and which may be communicated between human beings and/or computers for eventual retrieval by humans in intelligible form'. This could cover everything from hand-painted hieroglyphics to a computer-generated piece of videotape artwork.

The demarcation line between mail and messaging will always be narrow, probably defined by the purpose and urgency of transmitting the document rather than its size or complexity.

Urgent messages meant for recipients to act upon quickly are likely to be short, and of simple format. Consultative documentation, or material meant for participative co-authoring will more likely be long, of more complex layout and of lesser urgency – but not always.

A technical solution, or set of options, is required covering all combinations of requirement at the most cost-effective level. Currently available options, and advice about selecting from these, with appropriate human-oriented controls and priority levels, are contained in this section.

6.3.1 Technical options

The options currently open for sending text in electronic form include:

- telex: the tried and trusted international standard way to send messages or quite long documents with contractual validity, and to engage in two-way conversational exchanges in text over an open wire. Its limitations include speed (about 66 words a minute for most international connections) meaning cost, and the fact that text can only be printed out in upper case, since there are only five holes in the punched tape with which to achieve the necessary variants of character code

- teletex: an emerging super-telex service, with terminals having full word processing capability and able to address and print something over 300 different characters to international standards. Limitations of teletex are the fact that it is uni-directional (i.e. users cannot converse directly back and forth) in its basic implementations, and is single-page rather than document-oriented
- teletext (with the 't'): or what is sometimes called 'downstream selective' broadcasting of information in a continuous cycle over a TV channel, to be picked off one TV frame at a time for viewing by the end user. This system can be quite economical for in-house use as a *central* message-passing or broadcast information system, but will be less attractive if the requirement is primarily for passing individual messages between individual work-stations
- videotex: another type of system again taking advantage of TV channel capacity, but where the user makes 'upstream' inquiry of a database and the retrieved information is addressed direct to his video terminal. This inquiry be made of public or commercial databases connected to the system, or users can have what are known as 'private closed user groups', by which they can set up and update small or large numbers of private pages which can only be used by people with access to a videotex system who know the corporate code. This can be a very effective method of passing information quickly: for example price change information within a large organization's sales force. Its principal limitation is the need for a fairly expensive interface to the TV set
- mainframe maildrops: any organization with a medium-to large-sized central communicator, or network of computers with reasonably available storage capacity can set up a 'mail-drop' service by which messages or documents can be 'parked' in pre-determined files for collection at leisure by addressees who periodically inspect the contents of their mail-box
- information retrieval systems: can be used in a slightly more dynamic mailing role for some applications, by sending a short

message to interested parties of new documentation recently entered in the retrieval database
- special-purpose mail and messaging systems: based around mini-computers dedicated to storing and forwarding messages on demand, often with highly portable printer terminals connected in dial-up mode
- inter-communicating word processors can be used directly between each other to transfer complete documents for printout, or re-working on the receiving machine
- communicating word processors can be integrated into more complete office systems networks, in which the information their users require to send can be directed to the required addressee(s) through network control mechanisms rather than a simple one-on-one dial-up. Documents are placed in a notional out-tray for transference to a similar electronic in-tray in the receiving machine, and can be checked in and out in much the same way as conventional recorded delivery.

6.3.2 Control mechanisms

Before deciding on the technical option(s) to adopt, the prospective end user of electronic mail should sit down for some time and think first of the ways in which the people in the organization will most probably find it easiest to communicate.

- Will they need, for example, acknowledgement of the delivery of mail or messages, and does this need an immediate personal reply or is it enough simply to be assured by the system that it has delivered?
- What levels of priority should be allowed, bearing in mind that any priority higher than normal is liable to be degraded, without strict controls, because people generally tend to believe that what they have sent is more important than anything else in the pipeline?
- How confidential will mail be, and will some (or possibly all) of it need to be protected against intrusion or possible corruption *en route*?
- To what extent should receivers of the mail be able to change its contents (e.g. on word processors receiving documents in electronic form), or should they only be able to see a printed or displayed record?
- If the system should fail, how acceptable (or feasible) will it

be to regenerate everything from scratch and start again, or does fail-safe alternate routeing of communicated information need to be assured?

Once all these questions are answered, then the system can be designed around a suitable technology and there are enough options and variations for the solution to come fairly close to most needs (always provided the price is right).

6.4 PROCESSING THE SPOKEN WORD

Audio dictation of text, using magnetic tape or disk recorders to capture the human voice in analogue form, has been widely practised in offices for the past 30 years.

Copy typing from audio input is substantially enhanced, from both dictator and typist viewpoint, by the introduction of WP systems allied to the audio process. Dictated material is invariably a first draft, subject to corrections resulting from author change of mind, stylistic considerations and often mishearings, in addition to the usual error quotient for typed material. Audio typing using conventional machines has therefore frequently been felt to be the worst type of secretarial drudgery. For the author, too, the iterative correction process has often been unacceptably tedious.

Using a WP machine, the typist is suddenly in a position where the bulk of what is keyed is immediately re-usable without further effort on her part. Hitherto infuriating practices, such as the far from infrequent instruction to erase the last three or four sentences just after the typist has finished keying them, are far less of a problem. The author gets the first draft faster, knows it can be corrected quickly, can be less inhibited in asking for further changes. He/she also has the important advantage of knowing that no new errors will be introduced at the second and subsequent draft stages.

The combined use of centralized audio dictation systems and pooled typing units has been shown to be particularly powerful. The resulting improvement in throughput speed and presentational quality can induce authors who would not normally accept either dictation or pool typing to do so with gratitude. A further step in polishing performance is open to those with advanced, computer-controlled central audio, allowing the routeing of incoming audio direct to selectable typing stations. Assuming that a centralized WP system will have some form of activity monitor, it is possible to envisage future centralized systems where audio input could be automatically channelled to lightly loaded typing stations.

The ability to store audio messages and direct them to selected receive stations, in the same way as physical and electronic mail, is an important new development in office systems potential. Several suppliers now offer (or at least promise) such a facility, using digital compression techniques to reduce to a minimum the amount of disk space taken up by the recording. Even with such compression techniques, however, storage limits can quickly cause problems. The human voice normally requires a data-sampling rate of around 60 kilobits/second to achieve parity of digital and analogue tone quality. Compression to reduce this down beyond 9.6 kilobits is difficult, and a leading supplier estimates that 60 minutes' dictation and associated control data currently occupy some eleven *megabytes* of disk on his 800-megabyte system, which, with talkative users, could be short of storage within a few days.

The size of voice 'document' which might be transferred is enormous by comparison with its keyed-text equivalent; this has significant implications for the configuration of systems attached to any network, to prevent larger units transmitting more information than others can readily accept. It is also debateable whether the transmission of very large voice-only documents is efficient in pure information-handling terms, or even culturally acceptable for most organizations. The ability to send and store short messages outlining the topic a seeker wishes to discuss with a not immediately available colleague would, however, certainly save considerable amounts of currently wasted time and misunderstandings.

Several suppliers have decided that a sensible compromise is to provide for the treatment of small amounts of digitized voice as documents, particularly in attaching voice comments to keyed text. This appears to work well technically and to be generally acceptable from an organizational culture viewpoint. Voice synthesis also seems likely to play an important part in systems of the late 1980s. Speaking clocks, the widely used training toy which teaches children how to speak English with a Japanese accent and spell American-style, and other commercially available devices have made everyone familiar with the potential of chip technology to provide a reasonably credible emulation of the human voice.

Some office systems suppliers have announced plans to use voice synthesis to read out text databases over the telephone dial-up inquirers, and the feasibility of this is already well established in their laboratories. Voice recognition, i.e. making human speech intelligible to a computer, is much more difficult. Nonetheless, systems are already well established which can handle with acceptable accuracy numeric and command-type input from the human voice. Any office application, such as information retrieval, for example, which can be defined in a tightly structured environment may be performed by voice recognition systems in the near future.

Particularly attractive applications will be those in which the user cannot use a normal keyboard, such as in chemical laboratories, for example, where he/she needs to be doing other things with his/her hands at the same time as retrieving information.

Remote inquiry from the telephone handset, coupled with synthesized replies and procedural instructions from the computer, has already demonstrated its worth in a spare parts ordering operation by a British car manufacturer.

Recent developments, using the constantly growing power of the microprocessor to the full, have made it increasingly simple, and substantially cheaper, for a machine to recognize individual human voice patterns, and to filter out confusing background noise. But, however good at recognizing speech elements a computer may become, its interpretation of free-text semantics must remain debatable for some time to come.

A classic test for the all-speaking computer of 2000 or thereabouts will probably still be the telephone call home saying: 'I'll be late, I'm playing a round on the way home'. The wife presumably knows he is a golfer, the computer might reach quite different conclusions. It is also debatable whether the constraints of punctuation will make voice recognition easily acceptable in the office environment.

It is already difficult, and takes at least a week's training, in most organizations to get executives to accept the disciplines of orderly dictation.

Asking them to accept another fortnight's lessons in phonetic punctuation *à la* Victor Borge would probably overstrain staff relations somewhat.

6.5 MANUSCRIPT AND 'OFFICE GRAPHICS'

If handwritten information were universally legible, it is debatable whether the office typewriter would have needed inventing. If it could be read by many at one time, who would have needed the photocopier? But handwriting is not standardized, is often hopelessly unintelligible to anyone other than its author (and sometimes not even him/her after a few days have passed), and needs a physical recording medium.

Scanning manuscript by machine, and translating the sundry squiggles into standard encoded text is not yet a practical proposition, although there are machines which will recognize capital letters printed with reasonable care by hand in pre-defined boxed areas. The variations and possible combinations of most people's handwriting are still too great to make it feasible, or in any way cost-effective to harness computer power to the translation task. But it *is* possible, and several suppliers of office systems are now working in this direction, to scan the overall images of written words or documents and store them as pictures, with retrieval information attached so that they can be summoned to a high-quality display screen like any keyboarded text.

There are two difficulties with this approach:

(a) cost of storage, many times greater than the keyed equivalent, even with substantial data compression for the stored image
(b) printed output, requiring a hybrid, facsimile oriented printer if manuscript is to be mixed with typescript.

Compression techniques may be expected to alleviate but cannot be expected to eliminate the first problem; alleviation will be enhanced by the steady and continuing reduction in data storage costs. The second problem is increasingly susceptible of resolution by the emerging new generation of laser and LED printers, able to print anything which can be transmitted to them as a stream of information to control and form the lines of minute printed dots which they use to build up images of characters and graphic elements alike.

While the problems of capturing, storing, retrieving and printing out such graphic images cost-effectively may soon be resolved, communicating them to other systems and sites, espceially over low-capacity channels, poses another set of problems. Here again, it is to be expected that the reducing cost of technology will help, but the economics of communicating images will always be subject to the tarification policies of communications carriers. In order to transmit free-form pictures at acceptable speeds, a lot more bandwidth will always be needed than for coded characters, and this will have to be paid for. Recognising this, many suppliers and researchers have been progressively developing techniques for encoding graphic elements in standard form (see standards).

For the office, the most important developments will concern what may be described as 'office graphics', i.e. special symbols added to the standard national character set (such as the degree sign for temperatures) and simple shapes and curves such as those found on a standard flow-chart template. These elements will increasingly be encoded and transmitted to flexible printers with sufficient intelligence to store expanded character/symbol and shape sets in memory, and drive their print elements satisfactorily to print them out on receipt of the coded expression of those characters and elements. The printers to do this will be based on the principle of raster-scanning used for many years in wirephoto, facsimile printing, and television systems, i.e. building up an image as a series of lines of very small dots streamed rapidly and serially across a recording or display medium. For free-form graphic images, these machines (with needle-matrix, laser, LED and possibly thermal heads, (see hardware section) will work as though they were facsimile receivers. When receiving coded characters, their local microprocessor will extract from memory the information necessary to build up the characters or standard graphic elements whose coded expressions are being transmitted down the line.

7

Development strategies and tactical planning

Telecommunications and computing technology and skills have converged rapidly over the past decade to the point where it may be said that machine is finally beginning to emulate Man in terms of integrated information processing.

As a first step to establishing an *Information Systems Strategy,* it should, therefore, be decided to use this all-embracing title for long-range planning.

Information should be formally defined in this context. A suggested definition might be: 'data so structured that they are immediately recognisable as a means of transferring knowledge between humans. Such information may be in the form of written or printed alphanumeric text or standard symbols, graphic images of varying complexity, and audio-visual recordings'. (This will sit well with the definition of a document contained in section 6.3).

In the same way that commercial planners tend to develop their financial plans and targets as the periodic numerical expressions of central corporate aims, the information systems planner(s) should proceed to set down the *functional* aims of corporate information systems in a short, very simple statement couched in layman's language. This conceptual definition, constantly updated as needs and people change, should be regarded as the central core of the long-range strategy. Its interpretations, in more technical terms of both human and machine information systems, should similarly be maintained on a rolling basis. Major updating exercises should be embarked upon at least once every year, and preferably at six to eight monthly intervals.

Use of a WP system is *essential* for this task and other information systems planning documentation. The implementors must (a) be able to keep all interested parties fully informed, (b) put up a good presentational image in all their supporting documentation, and (c) be manifestly seen to take their own prescriptions, with beneficial effect.

7.1 FROM TACTICS TO STRATEGY

It will be neither possible nor desirable simply to announce a grand strategy and seek to impose it. In any organization, such changes cannot be made overnight. Progress towards an Information Systems Strategy must needs be evolutionary rather than revolutionary.

A *phased approach,* blending a tactical accommodation with the current state of information services into longer-term thinking, is the answer. The critical step in Phase I will be finding the first Custodian of the Strategy. This function ought, preferably, to be fulfilled by a full-time member of the administrative support staff, with a title something like 'Director of Information Systems'. Ideally, he or she should have extensive background experience in office automation, data processing and telecommunication; preferably with several years' experience in information storage and retrieval, reinforced by skill in organization and methods, operational research and behavioural science. In the perhaps not unlikely event that such a paragon proves difficult to find, initial custody of the strategy should be entrusted to a small group of two or three specialists, possibly including and certainly supported by external consultant effort.

The first task in establishing this new Directorate will be to write a clearly expressed job definition for the Director, or at least a charter for the Information Systems Directorate; this will be directly derived from the conceptual definition of an Information Systems Strategy. The Directorate should then proceed to execute a number of short-term tasks preparatory to making a start on long-range planning.

7.2 SHORT-TERM TASKS

To establish necessary short-term solutions which will be compatible with an eventual grand strategy, while coping swiftly with possible time-critical situations, a number of short-term tasks must be undertaken. These tasks will include:

- charting information flows within the organization and between it and other organizations
- segregating information processing applications into those needing centralized treatment, those which may be distributed and those which could always be stand-alone.
- making an inventory of existing information systems, both traditional and computer-supported and including all text and data processing, telecommunications and audio-visual equipment
- analysing this systems inventory to establish a short-list of current leading suppliers, and determine which equipment is unlikely ever to be compatible with any other
- preparation of user-department guidelines for short-term system selection, as part of a gradual shaping of system facilities towards a more integrated future
- setting up the nucleus of an information systems support group; as a preliminary to this exercise, detailed job specifications must be written
- creating an authoritative mechanism for liaison with and procedures for control of suppliers of hardware, software and consultant effort
- developing standard technical documentation for procurement of hardware and software, including basic criteria for acceptance testing
- (once the above are effected) setting up a consultative group for system users and support staff; this will serve as a direct guide to the systems support group on user demands, help to forestall deviation from the eventual grand strategy and generally act as a safety valve. As a preliminary exercise, a functional charter for this user group needs to be written and a consensus on this reached among interested parties
- running of systems appreciation courses for senior managers and other indirect users likely to affect significantly systems procurement and usage.

Phase I represents something like two man-years of work, and should involve at least two, or (more probably) three people full-time over an elapsed period of about one year. One person should be dedicated at least 50 per cent of his/her time to educational activity, which will constitute the most easily visible (and hence promotional) activity of the Directorate.

7.3 LONG-TERM STRATEGY

Once Phase I is achieved, the Information Sytems Directorate should have made its presence well felt, and be in strong position to continue progress towards the establishment of a long-term strategy, in which development may be more directly controlled than diplomatically encouraged.

The strategy should be embodied in a centrally maintained document, held and updated on a word processing system (N.B. such a system will be virtually indispensable for Phase I activity.) Its content should be broken down into a number of major elements, including at least those listed below, although experience will almost certainly dictate that these be added to and differently grouped.

Planning for each element may be carried forward independently to some extent, *provided* always that changes planned under one head are not allowed adversely to affect those agreed under another.

The basic contents list should include:

(1) *Functional requirements*
- end user needs
- indirect user needs
- inter-connection
- structural implications of change
- human performance measures

(2) *Structural philosophy*
- electronic *vs* paper-work
- centralized systems
- semi-distributed
- stand-alone work-stations
- remote working
- network topologies

(3) *Systems standards*
- procurement
- acceptance testing and audit

– maintenance/support
– compatibility criteria
– communication protocols and formats
– machine performance
– documentation

(4) *Supplier policy*
– preferred short-list
– survival quotient
– evaluation procedures
– discount strategies
– non-standard systems

(5) *Support needs*
– information systems management
– hardware maintenance
– software support
– systems analysis
– development support
– consumables control

(6) *Development paths*
– compatibility optimization
– special-purpose work
– consultant involvement and control

(7) *Management considerations*
– cost-effectiveness
– semi-quantifiable benefits
– desired qualitative enhancement
– forward budgetary planning
– accommodation†

(8) *Security*
– confidentiality
– data protection
– idiot-proofing
– transmission integrity
– systems backup
– definition(s) of 'need to know'

†N.B. Space needs for central equipment will decline as component miniaturisation progresses.

Glossary of terms

This section contains a list of terms used in the first seven sections of this book, with a brief explanation in layman's terms of each. It is not intended to be an exhaustive dictionary of terminology used in connection with office systems, because (a) it would be difficult to know where to stop, (b) many frequently-used terms have a wide semantic spectrum, and (c) new expressions are constantly being taken up and old ones dropped.

ALPHANUMERIC – letters and numbers.

ARCHITECTURE – the way in which a computer system is designed to process information.

BIT – the basic unit of digital data, i.e. zero or one.

BUFFER – short-term memory used in a transient information handling activity, e.g. holding text input by keyboard and displayed on-screen before it is transferred to backing store, or storing text transmitted to a printer at high speed and feeding it at a lower speed to the printer.

BUS – a high-speed data transfer linkage between elements of a computer system.

BYTE – usually eight bits, normally denoting one character (*v.i*).

CRT – cathode ray tube (TV tube).

CHARACTER – a single unit of text (a letter) or numeric data (a number).

CODE-STRIPPING – a process for reducing the amount of information contained in one level of communications code so that it can be used at another; commonly used, for example, for eliminating the lower-case element of six- or eight-level code to make output suitable for five-level telex transmission (see under F). In the case of eight to five it is actually more conversion than stripping.

COMMAND – an instruction given by a system user to the system to perform a specified function.

CONCATENATION – chaining together (e.g. as of standard paragraphs of text, or system commands.

CONCURRENT RUN-TIME OPERATING SYSTEM – control system for a computer which allows several tasks to be performed (i.e. programs run) at the same time rather than one after the other.

CURSOR – an illuminated point of light on a CRT which moves as information is entered or edited, to indicate to the user exactly where he/she is working in terms of material displayed on the screen.

DISK – (usually spelled this way) a rigid disk of magnetic recording medium, usually encased in a cartridge or multi-disk pack, on which substantial amounts of digital data can be electronically written and retrieved or overwritten, using either fixed or moving read-write heads somewhat similar to a record-player pickup head, but not actually in contact with the recording surface.

DATABASE – a structured store of information.

DISKETTE – a flexible plastic disk in a thin protective jacket, more commonly known as a 'floppy disk', holding considerably less information than a hard disk, but cheaper per unit and more easily handled.

DOT MATRIX – a grid or matrix of dots within which a picture is built up; commonly used for displaying characters on a CRT, building up the outline of a letter for example from a series of vertical and horizonal illuminated dots.

DWELL TIME – the length of time for which an image will stay on a screen without being refreshed by a new bombardment of its internal surface by the electron gun of the CRT.

ELECTRONIC FILING CABINET – a term often used to describe the ideal office information retrieval system.

ELECTRONIC MAIL AND MESSAGING SYSTEMS (EMMS) – systems for transmission by electronic means of documents of varying length and urgency.

ETHERNET – a wideband local-area network concept implemented by Xerox and adopted by other suppliers.

FILE – a collection of records (electronic or conventional).

FIVE-LEVEL – commonly used to refer to the coding system used for telex transmission; Telex paper tape has up to five holes punched in it laterally per character transmitted, providing enough coding combinations to cover all alpha characters in upper-case only, all ten basic numerals and a limited range of symbols.

FOUNT – a range of characters available to be displayed or printed; drawn from type-*found*ers' (i.e. manufacturers of lead type) terminology and sometimes spelled 'font'.

GIGABYTE – 1,000 million bytes/characters; also gigabit (= 125 million bytes), gigahertz (= 1,000 million cycles/second) etc.

HERTZ – basic unit of oscillation frequency (1 Hertz = 1 cycle per second); CRT image refresh rates are commonly geared to the Hertz rate of the electrical power source.

HOPPER FEEDER – a device for feeding cut sheets of paper into a WP system printer; equipped with basic logic enabling its functioning to be controlled by the output software of the WP system.

INTERFACE – a linkage/meeting point, e.g. between different systems hardware or software elements, or at which man and machine interact.

INK-JET – a type of printer spraying ink onto paper to form characters or other images under logical control.

JOB – a quantity of work/information processed by a computer system.

JUKEBOX – a mechanism used for storing and retrieving information on a multiplicity of microfiche, optical disks or tape cartridge media; selection of the appropriate unit and its retrieval for 're-playing' the stored information works in the same way as the nickel-odeon (jukebox) coin-in-the-slot popular record player of the 1950s.

KILOBYTE – 1,000 bytes/characters, often referred to in abbreviated form as one 'K'; this can however get confused with kilobits and other uses of K as the shortened form of kilo.

KEYPAD – a small keyboard containing only a sub-set (often the numerics) of the range of characters found on a full WP or DP system keyboard.

LAN – local area network; a high-speed communications system linking a large number of devices to a variety of other devices.

LCD – liquid crystal display, of the kind used in electronic watches, consuming a very small amount of energy per character displayed.

LED – light-emitting diode; these are often assembled together in serial dot matrices to form line displays of characters, etc.

LIST PROCESSING – in WP terms, handling lists of items or names and merging them intelligently often supported by heavy sorting and selective extraction software; e.g. building and using specific interest-group mailing lists from within an overall directory of potential customers.

MEGABYTE – one million characters, usually abbreviated to MB; also mega*bit*, mega*hertz*, etc.

MENU – a list of actions open to a terminal user and displayed on-screen to help him/her perform allotted tasks. Selecting from these options (often by a single keystroke) will either issue a system command, summon the application program required, or take the user to another menu giving more specific help and advice.

MESSAGE SWITCH – a computer-based device for storing temporarily and forwarding as a complete unit an assembly of information defined as a message; this may be a short or long document, and sent to one specific addressee, or a variety of them.

MICROSECOND – one millionth of a second.

MILLISECOND – one thousandth of a second.

MODEM – modulator/demodulator, used to convert digital signals into corresponding analogue wave-patterns and back when communicating over conventional voice-channels

MTBF – mean time between failure (of a system or component).

MTTR – mean time to repair (of a system fault).

NEEDLE-MATRIX PRINTER – an impact printing device using print pins or needles to print characters on paper, in dot-matrix form

NANOSECOND – one thousand-millionth of a second (used for gauging large-processor working speeds).

OPTICAL SYSTEMS – microform (microfilm, microfiche) and laser-holographic systems in which information is microscopically recorded in analogue rather than digitally encoded form. The term 'optical disk' is increasingly used generically to cover mass storage devices in which information is stored as a serial stream of pixels (picture cells) scanned from the original object/document.

PHOTOSETTER – compression of phototypesetter, a computer-controlled system for producing print masters photographically rather than in cast lead type.

PACKET SWITCH – a computer telecommunication system which breaks information up into small 'packets' typically of about 40 characters each, and then shepherds these packets safely from sender to addressee, on whose system they are rebuilt into complete documents.

PROM – programmable read-only memory: i.e. a fast-access memory store from which data may be read but into which it cannot be entered, except by a complete re-programming (sometimes called 're-burning') exercise.

RAM – random access memory (i.e. memory store in which access can be directly gained to a given item of information rather than serially as with magnetic tape, for example); usually employed to refer to solid-state (i.e. chip technology) storage.

RASTER-SCAN – a technique of scanning images either to break them down and transmit them, or build them up to display/print them, involving very rapid movement of a scanning or print head across the area of image at very narrow line separations; the information is handled in serial lines. A typical example is the flying-spot scanner used to build up images on a home TV set, which 'writes' a 625-line picture 50 times a second on the screen.

RECORD – a basic set of information relating to some specific item, transaction or individual.

REFRESH RATE – the frequency with which an image on a CRT is refreshed (i.e. the information to rebuild the image is regenerated from screen buffer); this is frequently geared to the electrical frequency (i.e. 50 hertz in Europe).

RETRIEVAL – recovery of information from electronic or conventional storage media (or a mixture of both), by structured reference index, keyword, known content or free text search.

ROM – read-only memory (see PROM).

SCROLLING – the facility to move through text vertically or horizontally, using the screen as a 'window' onto text being rolled past it as though a scroll of paper were being wound through.

SORTING – rearranging lists of items or individuals by varying parameters, e.g. alphabetical order, postal code, section number.

STANDARD PARAGRAPHS – formally standardized elements of text assembled by pre-programmed and/or instance-specific commands in the classic WP application of building customized letters.

SUB-ROUTINE – a set of instructions which must frequently and repetitively be given to a computer system, and which are therefore assembled into a standard sequence, summonable by a more economically encoded command.

TABLE – list of information frequently used by a computer; often used in the context of a 'look-up' or 'translate' table, where the system automatically goes to look for instructions or conversion equivalents (e.g. when using different print elements on a multifount printer).

TAPE – magnetic tape, used for computers but essentially similar to that used for home tape recorders and players.

UPPER-CASE – capital letters, taken from the old printing trade, where a printer had one wooden, compartmentalised case for holding capitals, and another for small, LOWER-CASE characters. On a typewriter or word processor, upper-case is achieved by using a SHIFT key to denote the change from one case to the other.

VECTOR-PAINTING – a display technique in which, rather than building up an image one line at a time (see raster scan), the image is built up directly from point to point, with each point defined by a separate location vector (i.e. vertical and horizontal intersection).

WORD-WRAP (alternatively FULL-WORD WRAPAROUND) – a WP system facility preventing a word being broken or piling up at the end of a line, 'wrapping' it instead round onto the next line, without the need for a carriage return which would be required with a conventional typewriter.

WAN – Wide Area Network: a telecommunications network linking physically distributed locations.

XEROGRAPHIC – used of printing techniques employing the image transfer techniques developed by Xerox for photocopying.

Y-SWITCH – a hardware (and sometimes software) mechanism for allowing a peripheral device (usually a printer in the WP context) to be alternately used by two work-stations.

Index